Managing in the Educational Madhouse

A GUIDE FOR SCHOOL MANAGERS

David E. Hellawell

Dedication

To Dennis and Amy, the forerunners of the next generation.

The articles collected in this book were first published between 1997 and 1999 in *Managing Schools Today* magazine, published by the Questions Publishing Company, 27 Frederick Street, Hockley, Birmingham B1 3HH.

ISBN 1 84190 011 7

Edited by Brian Asbury
Designed by Al Stewart
Illustrations by Iqbal Aslam, Paul Dainton and Alex Hughes

Printed in Great Britain

Other titles by David Hellawell also available from Questions Publishing:

The Headteacher from Hell and Other Animals
ISBN 1 898149 62 3

Total School Mis-management
ISBN 1 898149 31 3

Contents

About the author

Since his last humorous book, the author has taken official retirement from full-time work (although scholars are still debating the exact date at which he took *unofficial* retirement from full-time work, and some over-academic pedants maintain that he never actually engaged in full-time work at any point in his so-called career). He is now Emeritus Professor of Education Management at the University of Central England in Birmingham. He is also known to take money from such agencies as the Open University, the European Commission and the Church of England. It is less clear whether these worthy bodies are aware of this. In addition, the writer undertakes management consultancy contracts in a variety of organisations in various European countries outside the European Union (EU). He is very much in demand in what are referred to in Brussels as the 'aspirant countries' of Central and Eastern Europe, where his performance is such as to reassure these nations wishing to join the EU that they have nothing to fear about the managerial competence of those already operating within 'Fortress Europe'. The official motto under his distinctive logo is 'Have Degrees, Will Travel'.

Introduction

Writers and researchers on the debilitating aspects of stress in the workplace (and there can, of course, be positive effects of a certain amount of stress on motivation, etc.) usually advocate coping mechanisms of two differing categories. The first category is that of changes in the behaviour of the individual suffering the stress, and the second is that of changes in the organisational framework within which the individual operates (a search for prime causes that moves along a continuum from sick people, through sick buildings to sick organisations). I would like to suggest that there is a third category which bridges the other two, and this is to try to change the way in which the individual perceives that organisational framework. In the case of school managers, I want to show how a change in perspective about schools can be a very effective way of reducing stress levels and can certainly help to counter some of the more damaging aspects of stress.

This change in perspective moves away from a view of schools as organisations where rational human beings work in synchronised harmony according to prearranged blueprint plans, and on to a vision of schools as settings where irrational human beings spin past, and occasionally into, each other in a series of pirouettes on the rim of the volcano. (This is a similar metaphor to that which I now discover was first used by Alban Berg, the composer, when referring to the carnival crowds in Munich on the night of the Reichstag fire of 1933. This latter conflagration was used by Hitler as his justification for turning Germany into the totalitarian state which became, for many, a living nightmare.)

In short, this is a shift from seeing schools as places where you are surprised and dismayed if things go wrong, to viewing schools as locations where you are daily delighted and astonished if anything in the choreography goes right. If the image of dancing on the rim of the volcano seems somewhat fanciful, I would argue that it only expresses in metaphor what a lot of distinguished writers (together, no doubt, with a whole host of totally *un*distinguished writers!) have been saying about the world in general for a long time. One Will Shakespeare – he of the telling phrase – summed this world view up quite neatly in *Macbeth* where life itself is described as a tale told by an idiot, full of sound and fury, signifying nothing. This is not to argue that the views of one character at one point in one of the many plays necessarily sums up the total world view of the many-faceted bard, but there are great writers in our own century who have made it clear that they do indeed see the world as an arena where events which appear irrational or non-rational (and there is a difference) are the norm rather than the exception.

Resisting absurdity

Albert Camus, the Nobel Prize winner for literature of 1957, not only depicted the world as essentially 'absurd' throughout his *oeuvre*, but also showed how fiercely most human beings struggle to resist this interpretation. So, for example, death from 'natural causes' at an early age in one of his novels has to be explained away by those close to the deceased as the result of his excessive blowing of wind instruments! Ultimately Camus views as heroic the attempt to create your own meaning in the world while still clearly perceiving that world as essentially without meaning in itself; but it might equally be seen as a possible stress survival mechanism.

As far as everyday organisations are concerned, this perspective of the world as 'absurd' is often expressed colloquially when individuals talk about their daily round as being 'like working in a madhouse', and many of us have seen on office walls those posters to the effect that: 'You don't need to be mad to work here, but it helps!' Nevertheless, there is often an underlying assumption that this lunacy is a special feature of this or that organisation rather than the general rule. The fact that commercial firms find it profitable to mass-produce posters of this kind suggests otherwise.

In more recent times, chaos theory has emerged as a new attempt to explain a world which, it is assumed, will be to all appearances erratic, irregular and discontinuous. The idea of a linear, regular progression from plan to implementation is rejected by chaos theory, which takes for granted the idea that unpredictable consequences will inevitably intervene between the planning stage and the point at which outcomes become apparent. Chaos theory should encourage all managers to discard ideas of controlling the change process by sticking to immutable plans – as should the experience of Central and Eastern Europe with rigid Stalinist five year plans, which proved to be a total disaster for the economies concerned. This is not to say that all planning is futile, but that plans must be flexible, constantly monitored and constantly adjusted as unpredicted and seemingly irrational events occur (as they most certainly will).

Illusions of rationality

It is, however, very understandable (for reasons I will go on to elaborate) that headteachers are particularly prone to regard their own schools, and even those of others, as essentially rational in nature (from now on in this introduction I will use *headteacher* as a shorthand for anyone in a management position in schools). Indeed, heads of schools are often singled out for satire in this respect by those writers whose vision of the world is somewhat anarchic. For example, the Monty Python team in general were quick to prick the bubbles of headteacher pronouncements, which the team regarded as portraying authority in an excessively rational, not to say pompous, light.

One of the Python team, John Cleese (in the film *Clockwise*) also acted the part of a headteacher whose life of timetabled hyper-rationality came to a series of juddering halts once he had made the first slip by catching the wrong train to a heads' conference. Cleese was apparently bowled over by his first reading of Michael Frayn's film script, and in the light of Cleese's own creative preoccupations it is easy to see why he was attracted to acting out this particular head's obsessions. The character of Mr. Stimpson, the headteacher, is that of a 'control freak' – that is to say, someone who is obsessed with striving for an orderly perfection which, in the last resort, proves to reside only in his own neurotic imagination. He has an insight into the problem when Frayn puts the following words into his mouth: "I don't mind the despair; I can manage the despair. It's the hope I can't stand."

Too many heads have unrealisable hopes which, when things go seriously pear-shaped, can put them under excessive strain. Come to think of it, maybe the ultimate portrayal of an individual continually faced with the management of the absurd, but totally unable to comprehend this, is Cleese's tragicomic creation of Basil Fawlty. Fawlty, as Cleese himself has subsequently acknowledged, is a manager on the edge of a total nervous collapse. He totally lacks any insight into himself or the nature of management which could help him to cope with the regular exposure of the gap between the reality of running Fawlty Towers and his pathetic mental model of 'controlled' hotel management.

So why is it that heads are seen as so liable to catch this virus of hyper-rationality? Perhaps one of the reasons is that teachers as a whole display alarmingly similar symptoms. Outside observers of the teaching profession have often noted that teachers are great seekers after the 'right answer'. As Stanley Middleton wrote in *The Daysman*: "The trouble with schoolteachers is that they think all problems are soluble. They aren't." This may be partly linked to that potential professional deformity of teachers which is caused by continually asking questions to which they already know the answers (or at least think they do). This is *not* a normal human condition. However, some teachers seem unaware of that fact, and carry over this classroom practice into other informal social gatherings such as parties, with predictably dire results. Furthermore, it is in the very nature of teaching some school subjects that problems will be set by teachers which are indeed invariably soluble. As Middleton points out, problems in real life all too often have no solutions known to man or woman.

Puzzles and problems

Reg Revans, the guru of action learning, makes a useful distinction in this respect between managerial puzzles and managerial problems. You know in advance with puzzles as he defines them that they have right answers which can be found if you can only work hard enough and be smart enough. Problems, on the other hand, by his definition may or may not be soluble, and you have no advance knowledge of the existence or otherwise of a solution. Revans' argument is that although we may be given 'puzzles' to which we know there is a solution as part of a conventional management training programme, what we face in real life managerial situations are 'problems'. This forms part of his case against the artificiality of much of what purports to be management training.

As far as this disease of seeing all problems as potentially soluble is concerned, I think that although some teachers may have developed a particularly virulent strain, it is a virus to which much of the human race is susceptible. One of the great attractions of soap operas to their mass audiences on TV seems to be that they tidy up all the loose ends with rational – if not always entirely plausible – 'solutions'. One of the features of the German twin series of 'Heimat' programmes, which raised these series well above the conventional 'soaps' despite the superficial similarity of the format, was that events would occur for which no rational explanation was adduced. The loose ends of real life were scattered around the programmes. The degree of realism which this engendered made it blindingly obvious how unrealistic and artificial most soap operas are in this respect. No matter how complicated and troubled the lives of characters in *EastEnders* or

Brookside may be (and inferior soaps don't even have this degree of complexity), at least their 'stories' have beginnings, middles and endings that people can recognise as 'logical'.

Living backwards

This may be another reason why many people prefer to live in the past. Past events can easily be 'adjusted' with suitable *post hoc* rationalisations so that life appears to make a kind of retrospective sense – e.g. don't blow too hard into wind instruments! As the Danish philosopher, Kierkegaard, expressed it many years ago, it is much easier to understand life backwards, but unfortunately we have to live it forwards.

Post-modernist films such as *Pulp Fiction*, which do not follow the usual sequential patterns of older screenplays, appear to divide audiences along generational lines, with a greater tendency amongst the young to welcome what for many of them is a more realistic depiction of the way apparently random events confront them on a daily basis. Perhaps the downside of this reality has not yet, for the most part, hit them as severely as it has their elders, who often appear to react very unfavourably to such a presentation of 'real life'.

This kind of reaction may be also why the demagogue's big lie has often been seized upon so gratefully, but with such potentially disastrous consequences, by so many of the population at times when life seemed to them to be full of insoluble problems. Waltzing away with Hitler as a way of relieving the tensions of being on the rim of the volcano proved to be an illusory dash for security which turned into a dance with death. To paraphrase H.L. Mencken, for every difficult and complex problem there is one simple solution ... which is wrong! Would that all fundamentalists of whatever creed, cult or dogma had that dictum on their wall to gaze at for at least a moment or two each day!

Even accepting the fact that this tendency to look for 'the one right answer' may be part of the human condition in general, I still feel heads should be aware that their staff may be more prone to the malady than some other sections of the population, for the reasons I have already advanced. This can put a lot of pressure on heads, who are inevitably not going to come up with magic answers to all a school's problems no matter how hard they work and how intelligently they manage. This is not to deny the virtues of hard work and smart management, but it makes the point that from time to time life has a nasty habit of smacking managers in the face, or tripping them up on banana skins, no matter how well they manage. (Remember the Monty Python foot which periodically squashed various stout parties in mid-flow?)

So heads might well take to heart the management concept of 'satisficing'. This is not just another example of how management gurus can mangle the English language. It is intended to convey the meaning that, for most of the time, managers will not come up with perfectly 'satisfactory' answers to the managerial problems they face, but will have to make the best of a very imperfect job and go for what they judge to be the optimal solution at the time.

Acquiring a halo

To look on the bright side (to continue the Pythonesque strand), if enough of these 'solutions' come close enough to satisfying most of the clients most of the time, the fortunate head may acquire the reputation of being a shrewd manager. Once this halo is acquired, it can take a lot of misfortune to shake it off. It is surprising how often the actions of the 'shrewd manager' will be subjected to *post hoc* rationalisations to 'prove' that what seemed like a seriously daft decision at the time was actually all part of a devilishly cunning plan whose outcomes will only manifest themselves in the longer term (and those who crave certainty and security in this world will go to no end of trouble to try to maintain the illusion thereof).

Heads may well wish to create such propaganda on their own behalf, but they should never fall into the trap of actually believing it themselves. For there will be times when mistakes are made, and, more importantly, when no mistakes are made at all, but the world still collapses around your ears in any case. I write this long after the very school used for the location shooting of *Clockwise* suffered a major fire which I am perfectly sure the head concerned could not have prevented, no matter what precautions he had taken.

There will be school closures in future which I am also sure will not, in many cases, be the direct result of poor management but rather the consequences of a bad roll of the demographic dice or whatever. As long as heads bear in mind that ultimately they are attempting to manage the absurd, and accept that fact with a certain degree of stoicism and a robust sense of humour, they may be better equipped to survive the stresses of this imperfect world. As John Lennon once memorably wrote: "Life is what happens to you while you're busy making other plans." (In the light of his own subsequent murder by a gunman clutching a copy of *The Catcher in the Rye* he could equally well have begun that sentence with the word 'death', which perhaps underlines the absurdity which this preface has been all about.)

In that sense, this is a book about everyday life in education management.

Hearing a different drummer

Henry David Thoreau is described in my antique version of *The Oxford Companion to English Literature* as 'a revolutionary and something of a wild man'. He was, then, perhaps well qualified to write that 'if a man does not keep pace with his companions, perhaps it is because he hears a different drummer. Let him step to the music which he hears, however measured or far away'. I am beginning to wonder if those of us managing 'wild' men and women, who exist in the world of education as elsewhere, would do well to heed those words a little more carefully than we appear to be doing.

Now let's get this straight. I am not against efficient and effective management in education. Some of my best friends are efficient and effective managers. What I am arguing is that really efficient and effective management can not only cope with, but actually allow to flourish within their organisations, the maverick, the unusual and even the occasional truly eccentric individual.

When I now look back through the mists of time (but not nostalgia) to my own schooling as a pupil, I doubt very much if I am being exceptional when I state that the teachers I remember most vividly as having had a lasting effect on me and my subsequent career are those who certainly appeared to be hearing a different drummer than most of the other teachers. In particular I will never forget a teacher by the name of B.A. Giles (whose initials could have been designed for schoolboy jokes), who was the first teacher of English I encountered at sixth form level. (I have to apologise to the primary school world that my personal memories of anything at all from that age as a pupil have always been of the very haziest. Maybe this is the case with politicians also, or they wouldn't come out with such claptrap about the wonders of the 'back to basics' education they received at that age. I can just about remember enough to tell me those were not the happiest days of my life.)

Ugh!

We had the kind of 'posh' sixth form where they started marking essays on the alpha, beta, gamma system and I well remember being very surprised indeed to receive my first sixth form essay back marked as gamma. This was not what I was used to, and furthermore there were various red biro annotations in the margin which said: 'Ugh!' This was not an expression I had come across in written form before and it was some time before I realised it was not pronounced 'Ugg'. It was a good few 'ughs' further on before I realised that B.A. Giles (I never knew his first name) was signifying by this annotation that he considered my essays to be liberally peppered with the kind of sentimental clichés up with which he would not put.

It was Ernest Hemingway who memorably wrote: "The most essential gift for a good writer is a built-in, shockproof bullshit detector." It was a tragedy that, in my own humble view, his own crap detector stopped functioning correctly in the latter part of his writing career. (If you don't agree with that example, you must accept our old friend William Wordsworth as a case in point where the detector went absolutely haywire in the later years.)

Most of us never aspire to those literary peaks, but even toiling in the foothills we need an inner voice which tells us when we're writing badly. B.A. Giles certainly fixed me up with a rudimentary prototype whose present efficacy only you, dear reader, can judge.

He was a great teacher of a kind I had never experienced before, because he conveyed world-weariness rather than enthusiasm. But it was a weariness with the dross in life, and that was something worth conveying. (He probably had every right to be world-weary because we picked up on the grapevine during the course of the year that he had some kind of incurable illness, and he did indeed leave the school at the end of that year.)

He was also a poet, and he was certainly the first person I had ever encountered who I was aware had actually had his work published. I strongly suspect, however, that his languid approach to teaching English literature would not have scored highly on any Ofsted tick list. Indeed, I am reminded of that spoof critique of the teaching of Socrates which went something along the following lines: 'is unkempt in appearance; appears to rely far too heavily on one teaching approach; is often rude and sarcastic when addressing pupils; etc.' A classic profile of a failing teacher. I wonder how one Christ J. would have fared in an Ofsted inspection, by the way? 'Relies too heavily on obscure parables in mixed ability teaching situations; should use more visual aids etc. Teaching = Grade 5. Unsatisfactory.'

Threats

No educational organisation could function effectively if all the staff were of the B.A. Giles variety, but the odd creative nonconformist has enlivened many a generation of school pupils. An ex-colleague of mine used to recall with delight one of her teachers who was fond of jump-starting any of his flagging pupils by diatribes along the following lines: "If you get that wrong again, I'm going to tear off your arm and beat you over the head with the bleeding stump." This was hardly anatomically accurate and would not, I suspect, have gone down too well in a court of law ("and then it is alleged, m'lud, that the accused said..."). But the point was, according to my informant, that his pupils all loved him as a teacher and revelled in his bizarre and outlandish threats, which one and all realised were flights of surrealist fantasy. The essential fact that they grasped was that he actually liked his pupils, despite (or perhaps because of?) the grotesque language which he employed in his relations with them.

The problem with the notion of the standard delivery of a standard curriculum is that it lacks the human element which can transform teaching into that 'something special' which stays with people over the years. I can still remember the enthusiasm with which one exiled Scot taught us to appreciate the writing of another of his compatriots (who also spent much of his life in England) through a reading over weeks of James Boswell's *Journal of a Tour to the Hebrides*. Not the most easily accessible of books for 14 year olds, but by Heavens he made it come to life for us. A strong desire to visit Scotland and to find out more about Sam Johnson were other lasting spin-offs as far as I was concerned. I wonder whether he would now have found the opportunity or the space, inside or outside the National Curriculum, to teach about something so clearly close to his heart?

Brodie

My experiences as a pupil at a single sex secondary boys school inevitably rule out any reminiscences about extraordinary female teachers, of whom there were none in my field of vision at that time. However, this prompts me to refer to that phenomenal fictional pedagogue, Miss Jean Brodie, depicted in her prime by Muriel Spark, who must have surely had some ex-teacher(s) in her mind's eye when she came to write that delightful novel. Even in the period depicted in the novel, the eponymous Miss Brodie had her little local difficulties with the powers that be; nowadays, though, I couldn't see her emerging successfully from any appraisal which attempted to set her performance targets linked to the school development plan.

Teachers like Jean Brodie are a law unto themselves, and any attempt to constrain them within the narrow confines of lesser mortals would be counter-productive. In real life, one hopes that her pupils, in their post-school days, would have sifted through her words of wisdom with extreme care – but they would surely never have forgotten her teaching during the years in which they were constantly informed that they were '*la crème de la crème*'.

There is, after all, good management research evidence to

suggest that effective teams require at least one creative ideas person in their ranks. Teams made up entirely of efficient completer/finishers or company workers (to use just a couple of Meredith Belbin's terms for typical group members) are unlikely to contain that vital spark which the successful team needs. Belbin originally used the term 'plant' for the ideas merchant because he and his co-workers discovered that it was essential to plant such a person in a group if the members were collectively going to deliver the goods as a successful team. Teaching teams, like any others, need the kind of person who is prepared suddenly to shout out "A crocodile! A crocodile!" in the midst of a perfectly serious staff meeting. (This is not a product of the realms of fiction, I assure you; the intervention, bizarre as it seemed at the time (and still does!), was actually the precursor to a brilliant solution to a seemingly intractable problem by a somewhat eccentric member of staff.)

Iconoclasts

All managers should learn to live with the creative iconoclast(s) in their midst if they really want truly effective educational organisations (although it is certainly legitimate and pardonable to pray fervently that there aren't too many). It's the B.A. Gileses of this world who help to develop creative and critical thought on the part of their pupils.

In my bleaker moments these days, I sometimes have a feeling that the Government is determined to drive out such teachers in favour of a docile and conformist teaching 'workforce' which will 'deliver' the National Curriculum in such a way as to produce further generations of pupils who are equally good at following instructions handed down from above. This might have some pay-offs for those in high authority who do not want to have an active and thoughtful citizenry who might actually be critical of government measures, but I shudder to think what it will do in the longer term for a nation which is increasingly going to have live on its creative and imaginative wits if it is to prosper economically. It's worth remembering the words of Friedrich Nietzsche which roughly translate as: 'You need a little chaos in your heart to give birth to the dancing star.' Here's to the managers of schools who are prepared to pay the undoubted price in order to allow the dancing stars to continue to illuminate our lives.

Lies, damned lies and interviews

AT AN early stage in my career in education I well remember a discussion with some fellow young teachers in the school staff room when all but one of us were bemoaning the stress involved in applying for jobs, and in particular in facing interview panels. The one exception said that he rather enjoyed interviews and didn't experience any tension. When we asked how he coped with especially difficult questions about his capabilities in this or that respect, he replied: "Oh I just lie. I lie all the time in interviews."

This certainly took me aback at the time and I still marvel at his *chutzpah* because, as Quintilian said a very long time ago, to be a convincing liar you have to have an exceptionally good memory. In my own research interviews, for example, it is very easy to spot what I would prefer to regard as inconsistencies when the interviewee is posed what is essentially the same question in different guises over an hour and more of interview; but I suspect that in the standard job interview it is a good deal easier to pull the wool over the eyes of the interviewers. The only problem then is what happens if you get the job and somebody takes you up on your false claims?

Wild claims

Exactly the same problem must face the applicant who gets a job partly on the false pretences of claims in his or her CV. 'First sponsored blindfold ascent of the North Face of the Eiger on behalf of Save the Children' may be a difficult claim to check out at interview, but just suppose the applicant gets the job and is put in charge of the school rock climbing club? If you are, by the way, under the impression that CVs can be accepted at face value, you are a good deal more trusting than many commercial firms these days. There are actually private agencies that now make their entire specialist livings (and very good livings they are too) out of commissions from firms to check out the validity of the CVs they receive from job applicants.

But, strange as it may seem, circumstances at interviews can sometimes dictate that the applicants have a vested interest in presenting as unflattering a version of themselves as possible. A colleague of mine once received, by coincidence, invitations to interviews in two different schools on the same day in the same town (at the other end of the country from where she was based). Fortunately, or otherwise as things turned out, one was for the morning and one for the afternoon, so it was possible to reply that she would attend both sets of interviews.

At the end of the morning interviews she was offered the job in the first school, which she favoured in any case. At this point she was honest and naïve enough to say that she would almost certainly take the job but she had promised to attend another interview in the afternoon, so she would only confirm after this had taken place. The head, who was well ahead of her time in cost consciousness, said words to the effect of: 'Fine. In that case we will pay one half of your travel and accommodation expenses, and the other school can pay the second half.'

It was only when she had left the school that my friend realised the full nature of the dilemma she faced. If she now did equally well in the afternoon interviews and was offered the job there as well, she would only have to turn it down in favour of the first school. This would give the second school the perfect right, which they would undoubtedly exercise, not to pay any expenses at all. But this would be equally the case were she now to withdraw from the interview.

Beelzebub

At a time in her early career where every penny counted, the prospect of being paid only half her expenses did not exactly appeal. Therefore there was really only one strategy left open to her – she had to attend the second interview and make absolutely sure she was seen as a totally unacceptable applicant. One can only imagine the kind of interview dialogue that might ensue:

Q. Do you like children?
A. Very much so, especially when garnished with hollandaise sauce.

Q. Are you available after school hours for extra-curricular activities?
A. No, because that would affect my evening work as a barmaid.

Q. Are you prepared to teach RE?
A. Absolutely. My lord and master, Beelzebub, is always on the lookout for new disciples.

. . . and so on. Suffice it to say, my colleague was not offered the post.

The above interview dialogue is, I hope, fictitious, but I assure you that the following interview exchange is as close to the actuality as possible, because I was the interviewee in question. It goes to show that speaking the most unpalatable truth can on very rare occasions be a winning strategy in interviews. Some background to the exchange is essential to explain what subsequently took place. At one point in my career I had decided to leave school teaching and go for a lectureship in teacher education. Rightly or wrongly, I felt myself to be a very marketable commodity as far as the higher education (HE) sector was concerned. I applied to a variety of HE institutions and fairly quickly received two invitations for interviews at a university and a college of education. Unfortunately from my point of view, the latter interview, for a post which I regarded in status terms as the inferior of the two, nevertheless came chronologically first.

This job did have one potential advantage, however, in that it was advertised at 'lecturer/senior lecturer' level. There was no doubt that if I were accepted at the latter level I would be much better off financially than I would be in the university post. As the sole crust-winner, with a young family, I could not afford to discount the possibility of the higher income. I therefore duly turned up at a rain-swept railway station in the Yorkshire town where the interviews were to take place the following day. I wasn't into paying for taxis in those days (and neither were colleges), so I enquired where the college was, to be told it was 'just up't road'. 'Just up't road' turned out to be one of those Yorkshire understatements I was soon to know and love.

Derelict

The college was, in fact, perched high on a Pennine hilltop surrounded by parkland on that well known early twentieth century principle that the young 'gels' in teacher training needed protection in rural isolation from the rude townsfolk in the heavily industrialised valley below. By the time I got there I was not only comprehensively drenched, but I had been given a splendid opportunity to pass close by a number of the woollen mills on which the town's former prosperity had been based. I was not impressed. The derelict factories were undoubtedly the worst, but even those still running were belching out smokestack pollutants and it didn't require a premature eco-warrior to recognise that they might be seriously bad for your health.

I was given a tour of the college the following morning by staff who quickly informed me that if I had any illusions that I might walk straight into a senior lectureship I might as well forget them forthwith. Many of them had been queuing up for years for promotion to that level, and they assured me that adverts of the lecturer/senior lecturer variety were only used as bait for the unwary. So by the time I reached the principal's office for our preliminary chat, I was less than enchanted by the prospect of a job offer.

I was very quickly given the opportunity well and truly to burn my boats, because the good lady asked me for my impressions of the town in question 'now that I'd had a chance to look round'. I don't remember all the words I uttered over the next five minutes or so, but I do know that the expression 'dark satanic mills' was a recurrent leitmotif in my diatribe. To my utter astonishment, the principal became wreathed in smiles, left her desk, sat next to me and said: "Do you know, I used those exact words when I was interviewed on the radio about this town, and the local citizenry has been persecuting me ever since."

It transpired that she had been on a BBC programme then called *Down Your Way*, in which an interviewer named Franklin Engelmann, famous in his day, visited one town each week and interviewed the locals. In this case the locals had all extolled the homely virtues of their good town. The principal had not only been the sole interviewee to offer any criticism, but had done this as a 'foreigner' only recently domiciled there.

State of mind

All my readers who are familiar with Yorkshire will be well aware that it is not so much a geographical area but a state of mind – a state of mind best described as a bloody-minded chauvinist conviction on the part of the natives that their patch of earth is a paradise envied by all other right-minded people who have had the misfortune to be born elsewhere. Given these indisputable facts, I am still prepared to believe that the principle that just because you're paranoid doesn't mean people aren't out to get you definitely applies in this case. (See the next chapter for the sequel to this saga.)

I don't remember much of the rest of the 'informal' interview, or of the more formal one which followed and which seemed to me to be totally dominated by the principal (who treated the local councillors present as lackeys who would refuse to do her bidding at their peril). The upshot was, of course, that I was made the offer of a senior lectureship, which I was in no position to refuse.

I still have a sneaking suspicion that my success had less to do with my qualifications and experience than with my expressed contempt for the town in question. On the other hand, I would say that being in a state of mind where you don't really want the job anyway can give you certain strategic advantages in any interview. The trick is to make the interviewers think *they're* being interviewed by *you*. This unnerves them and they quickly become convinced that you're doing them a favour by even considering the position they're offering, which is manifestly at an inferior level for a person of your quality. Try it next time you're being interviewed. It's been a winner for me.

Teachers' democratic rights

THE POINT in my career when I moved from teaching in schools to teaching in higher education could hardly have been a more dramatic transition. As I now remember it through the swirling mists of time, I had been to the college for the interviews (as I related in the last chapter) on a rain-swept Yorkshire Pennine day, and I had very little physical memory of the place when I turned up at the entrance to the college grounds, some months later, on what I thought was the day before term was due to begin.

This was the late nineteen-sixties, and my young family and I had moved into a new house close to the college the day before. This was the first time I had set foot in the place in anything like decent weather, and the immediate surroundings now seemed surprisingly beautiful in the sunshine, with parkland all around, in sharp contrast to the inner city environment of the comprehensive I had just left in the Northeast. (The first of the two schools in the same part of that town in which I had spent my first eight years in teaching recently appeared in hand-held camera footage on TV, and was presented as a typical 'problem' school in the decaying urban environment of our time. I didn't think it was that bad at the time, but then I appear to have left a trail of destruction in my wake during my career; the college I am now about to describe was under the wrecker's ball on the last sad occasion on which I saw it!)

As I stepped on to the college drive that day, I became quickly aware that not only was this a very long drive indeed, but that it had large and expensive limousines parked along its entire length. Maybe I'd got it wrong and *this* was the first day of term, in which case I was making a very late entry. As I walked alongside them, I also couldn't help noticing that some of them had liveried chauffeurs sitting in them. Now I had some vague notions of having moved up in the teaching world but this was ridiculous. The idea of tutors being chauffeur-driven to deliver the odd lecture or two, before being driven back to the stately homes from whence they came, did seem a little bit out of my league.

Huddles

Nevertheless, I made it somewhat apprehensively to the front entrance of the baronial style building and found my way to the staff room, which was already packed with people in what seemed like various excited and noisy huddles. I had been given the name of one member of staff by a friend who had known him from boyhood, and so I asked the first person I could buttonhole where I might find him. He pointed out to me a tutor sitting in the corner of the room and obviously the centre of attention of one of the aforementioned huddles.

I waited until he had finished talking and then introduced myself. "Oh yes," he said, "Ron told me you were coming. We must talk, but not now, because I'm the next into the inquiry." And back he went into feverish conversation with his little coterie.

I returned to re-buttonhole the first chap with whom I had made contact and muttered something about: "And what is this inquiry?"

"You mean you don't know?" he replied. "It's the first day of the inquiry into the principal's management of the college."

And here we begin to get to the nub of this article, for I had stumbled unbeknowingly into a legal battleground sparked off

by the majority of the staff having petitioned the governors of the West Riding to sack the principal. Neither at my interview nor later had anyone given me the slightest inkling of this gathering storm (but it could be, of course, that her appointment of me was seen by the staff as the ultimate proof of her irrationality.)

The principal happened to be not only supported by her own union but was also very rich – in at least her late husband's right if not her own – and she was well able to employ the brightest and the best in the legal profession. QCs were thicker on the ground than I have ever seen them before or since. Hence the chauffeured limousines; so some of my more grandiose aspirations to a life of luxury in HE disappeared just as quickly as they had arisen – never to return, sad to say.

Legal manoeuvres

The whole of that term was overshadowed by these legal manoeuvres, and it was only some time later that the result of the inquiry vindicated the much relieved majority of the staff who had taken the very hazardous steps into the legal minefield. They would have been very much at risk financially if the result had gone the other way, their own union having been very equivocal about backing them. The principal departed from the scene, and so I never really experienced her in what the staff alleged was her full tyrannical and irrational flow.

Looking back, I now realise that she was perhaps one of the most prominent casualties of the democratisation of colleges of education which had taken place not long before I had made the move from school to college. I had never heard of the Weaver Report up to that point, but I soon understood that Toby Weaver, the civil servant who had chaired the committee which drew up the eponymous report, had indeed fully deserved his fifteen minutes of academic fame. 'His' report really had transformed the world of teacher education.

This is becoming an extremely long lead-in to the key points about schools which I want to make in conclusion, but it will be impossible to fully understand these points if I don't paint a little of the pre-Weaver picture in such colleges. They could be, and often apparently were, run as one-man (or more commonly one-woman) dictatorships in those days of single sex institutions, when the primary school teaching world was perhaps even more dominated by women that it is today.

I have subsequently heard enough anecdotes from those who lived through those days to believe that it was not only the students who feared for their lives if they transgressed any of the many written, and even more unwritten, rules laid down by such tyrants. Male staff could, in front of their colleagues, be peremptorily sent home as 'improperly dressed' if their roll-neck sweaters concealed their ties, to give just one pettifogging example. In the college in which I was employed, the allegations against the principal's conduct with staff and students were far more serious, and I worked with some colleagues who showed every sign of having suffered mental torments from which they were unlikely ever fully to recover.

Constitutions

What the Weaver Report did was to establish model constitutions for colleges which gave the staff some sense of statutory right to have a say in the running of the institutions in which they worked. The 'academic boards' which resulted were usually top heavy with the upper levels of the college hierarchy, but there were some places even for elected 'groundlings', one of which I became during my three years in the college. The boards were *de jure* chaired by the principals, but the theoretical notion was one of *primus inter pares* rather than *l'état c'est moi*. Of course, some principals were more willing than others to move into this brave new democratised world, and the tricks and subterfuges which some employed to shore up the former autocracies deserve at least an article to themselves.

Nevertheless, after some years in which skirmishes and rearguard actions left many bloodstains on the carpets, if not bodies strewn upon the battlefields, an uneasy truce was declared between even the most recalcitrant principals and most obdurate staff. There was a genuine, if faltering, attempt to run these educational institutions on non-despotic lines.

I would not wish to romanticise this brief flowering of collegial relations in higher education, because in my view it was not strong enough to survive the managerialist counter-reformation of the Thatcherite 80s and beyond (one would have to look now to some of the oldest of our universities to be certain of seeing residual outposts of genuine participatory democracy). Nor would I deny that in pre-Weaver days there were some college principals who were, by their own personal inclination, enlightened leaders who tried to make their staff feel as empowered as possible. But in those days there were no statutes to prevent principals from behaving like petty tyrants.

Question

The key point I want to raise from all this is to ask why have staff in schools in England and Wales never had this flowering of democratisation? Where is the legal constraint which could stop a head in an English school, for example, from deciding to discontinue staff meetings? What is there in the articles and instruments of school government to prevent a head from corrupting every staff meeting into a lengthy monologue or an unminuted harangue, with no right of comeback on the part of staff?

17

Before anyone suggests that nothing like this could ever happen in schools, or that such statutory safeguards are simply impractical, consider the situation in schools in Germany. School statutes in that federal state vary between the *Länder*, but staff in general do have statutory rights in these respects and thereby have a sense of some formally established right of participation in the running of the school. The Germans do, of course, have some small experience of dictatorships, which has resulted in constitutional safeguards at all levels. As one German colleague once said to me: "Germany has at only one period in its history had a national police force. Its head was called Himmler."

There are other countries – Spain, for example – where this democratic principle has been carried to a much greater extreme in some regions, with heads being elected by and from their colleagues with fixed term, but usually renewable, contracts. I am not advocating this here, because evidence suggests that it created as many dangers as it set out to avoid in the first place. Certainly, the initial post-Franco democratic euphoria on school management in Spain has been tempered by experience, but it is interesting to note that heads are still often elected to office by the 'School Council' (which is the highest representational and governing body of the school and includes the school secretary, representatives of the teachers, parents, students, administration and auxiliary services and the local council).

So surely, in the UK, at least *some* statutory safeguards against potentially dictatorial management by heads could be built into the new national regulations on school government which are being proposed as a replacement for the existing articles and instruments of government? It is not yet clear whether this legislation will include, for example, a clear statement as to the powers of heads *vis-à-vis* those of governors, but a legal clarification of their functions and responsibilities – and, perhaps above all, the limitations on those powers – is badly needed.

Reversing the flow

IN ALL of my long working life in schools and higher education, my colleagues and I have consistently been hectored and badgered (and various other 'ereds') by people outside education to learn about management from the business world. Personally, I have been only too happy to learn any appropriate managerial lessons on offer from industry or commerce, or from any other sources for that matter. Indeed, one of the disappointments of my career was being refused, by my own higher education (HE) management, the relatively small time off required to take up a free offer I had negotiated of a place on a management training course designed for managers in commerce and industry.

My superiors justified this refusal on the grounds that the course was 'inappropriate' for someone working in the field of education. I later found a way around this objection by enrolling on another management course which was, again, not designed for those in education, but which was actually run by my own institution of HE. This made it rather more difficult for my superiors (who, incidentally, I often felt would themselves have benefited from enrolling on some management training courses) to claim it was inappropriate.

There has since been a sea change about schools being receptive to ideas from business management. When I first began teaching education management courses some decades ago, there was a great reluctance from heads and other school managers to accept the notion that lessons from the commercial and industrial worlds were at all relevant when it came to improving management in education. Now, the pendulum appears to have swung to the point where the words of business management gurus are all too readily accepted as applicable to education lock, stock and barrel. We seem, in this respect, to have moved from outright hostility to risible gullibility, with no stopover at healthy scepticism. This, of course, has all been part of a central government push to make public sector organisations much more subject to the pattern of incentives found within the private sector 'marketplace'.

The reverse case

Notwithstanding any of this, I would like to make the reverse case for the private business sector learning lessons of management from education. After all, why should it be assumed that this particular information flow is only one way? Admittedly, eyebrows and objections have been raised whenever someone has been appointed from outside the world of education to manage an educational enterprise, but it has nevertheless happened spasmodically during my working lifetime. Indeed, with the full blessing of the TTA, several non-teachers have signed up for the training leading to the National Professional Qualification for Headship (NPQH) which started in 1997. The TTA seems to think this will bring in some free market entrepreneurs to ginger up the headship business. It is much more likely to bring in those middle managers from industry and commerce who have come to realise that they will never reach the top in their own worlds. Such men and women might quite fancy the attractive salaries on offer for heading up any school of sizeable proportions.

Much farther back in time, I recall Geoffrey Holroyde being appointed from industry as head of the Sidney Stringer School and Community College in Coventry back in 1971. As Holroyde himself wrote with characteristic understatement some time later:

'The appointment of the head was not universally welcomed'. He went on to itemise the nature of the opposition to the appointment of a non-teacher as head. This came from some of the LEA officers, the teaching unions and the staffs of two of the schools to be amalgamated into the new organisation.

The opposition was, however, overruled, and the appointment was one of the factors that led the Open University to choose Sidney Stringer as a case study for one of its earliest education management units. One idea implicitly present in the OU booklet appeared to be that since this man had come from industry there must be managerial practice occurring at Sidney Stringer which was superior to that in most schools – which were, after all, managed by mere ex-teachers!

Flavour of the month

Now I don't for one second deny that there were interesting lessons to be learned from observing the organisational theory and practice which Holroyde had brought with him from the business world he had previously inhabited. On the other hand, it is interesting in retrospect to note that the emphasis he placed at the time on Management by Objectives (MbO) now seems like yet another of those flavours of the month which so often and so quickly seem to degenerate into next month's top of the flops. Imported into the world of education, it seemed to spawn long lists of rather trivial and somewhat tedious 'targets' which appeared, to this outside observer, to be potentially disempowering for the teachers concerned. With the benefit of hindsight I can, of course, see that this was only an early prototype of some of the bureaucratic horrors to come in education.

There was also the mildly embarrassing fact that, just before the second of the two OU TV programmes was made, Holroyde made a couple of highly contested managerial decisions which were subsequently reversed. The events surrounding these decisions led some of the staff at least to conclude (not unreasonably in my view, on the evidence produced) that they had been cynically hoodwinked into thinking they were being consulted when a decision had in effect already been taken. As an exercise in the black art of pseudo-consultation it took some beating, and, worst of all, it broke the vital eleventh commandment of management that thou shalt not be caught out, for the head's cover was well and truly blown.

For many years afterwards that particular TV sequence must have been seen up and down the land as a case study in how *not* to manage effectively in education. And just as an aside, the two TV programmes can now also be used as an exercise in 'spotting the politician before she became famous', because the current Schools Minister, Estelle Morris, has a bit part as 'the probationary teacher'!

But let me again stress that there *were* also many very good ideas imported from business management into Sidney Stringer. The key point I want to make here is not that such managers transferred to education make mistakes like the rest of us, but that transfer in the opposite direction would not just have raised eyebrows – it would have been laughed out of court. In other words, at no time in my working lifetime have I ever been aware of even a single case of a manager from the world of education transferring sideways to manage in a major business outfit of any size (as opposed to starting up his or her own business from scratch – which *has* happened).

I am not actually advocating this, because I think that all managers benefit from having worked at various lower levels in the sector in which they manage. I am not convinced from the OU evidence that Geoffrey Holroyde, for example, really understood the nature of some of the problems teachers face. And even today, the very idea that business managers could learn anything from education managers is still unthinkable to many. But why should this be the case? Consider the following arguments:

Hierarchies

Schools (and HE institutions, for that matter) have traditionally had very flat hierarchies when compared, for example, to industrial concerns in this country. A friend of mine from student days returned to a major national industrial concern in the UK after many years in government research abroad. One of his first remarks to me about his new firm was that he could not get over the sheer number of its status divisions. From memory I think he had identified about eleven levels on the hierarchy and he was still counting at the time.

These levels were not just reflected in the size of the pay-packet or salary – far from it. As an example, he pointed to the fact that when he, as a manager, went to lunch he was not allowed to dine in the same canteen as those he managed. Furthermore, any conversation he might be having on the way to lunch with *his* manager also had to stop at that point because they, too, were allocated to different levels of eatery, which just happened to be on separate floors of a very tall building (and guess which one was on the upper floor?). It was also, he alleged, quite evident to all concerned that with increased status went different qualities of cuisine. Perhaps this was only the kind of mythology that such divisions were almost bound to engender, but things which people perceive as real are real in their consequences, to update a famous sociological dictum.

Admittedly the above is going back some years now, but

there was a report in the *Independent* on 14 July 1997 of a survey of 550 workplaces by the Manufacturing, Science and Finance (MSF) union, in which the following line occurred: 'Senior managers have separate dining facilities in almost one in five firms.' The report went on to itemise other 'perks' enjoyed by senior managers, including their own health insurance schemes, longer holidays, etc. MSF general secretary Roger Lyons was quoted as saying: "Until we move on from the Victorian style 'upstairs downstairs' segregation of facilities and benefits, how can we work together to meet the challenges of the next century?".

Indeed, delayering could hardly have enjoyed the vogue it has had in industry and commerce in recent years if there had not been some over-elaborated hierarchies to dismantle in the first place. Yet any headteacher in the land worth his or her salt could have taught our business managers that simple but vital lesson many years ago, if only someone out there had been listening.

Blinding

I accept that it's a good deal easier to avoid many of the problems of hierarchy in a relatively small primary school. Collegial relations have always been the norm in such schools. In what seemed to me like a blinding glimpse of the obvious, an American guru was recently quoted as saying that management has to behave in such a way as to convince those they manage that 'we're all in this together'. He argued that the military has learned that officers who plan battles from privileged positions miles behind the lines do not inspire loyalty in their troops (a point which the World War I *Blackadder* series on TV made in rather more amusing and perceptive ways).

The best managers in education always used to know this. I suspect, however, that some of the business management notions imported to schools in recent years have had a pernicious effect in this respect. 'Headteacher' used to mean, at least in part, what the title suggests – someone who is still seen as part of the teaching force but who has the ultimate managerial accountability to governing bodies, LEAs and the like. My current research suggests that heads are increasingly abandoning their classroom roles as the managerial responsibilities loaded on to their shoulders from central government down take up all their working hours and more.

Nor should this be viewed as a flight from the classroom by managers who take the first chance to dust the chalk from their clothes. I have recently interviewed heads whom I had interviewed a decade before in an earlier research project. Among their number were people who had been quite determined to resist pressures to relinquish their teaching, but even some of this group have now given up this particular struggle.

Buffering

With the decline of LEA managerial control has also come a reduction in its previous 'buffering' function between schools and the outside world. To use the kind of management terminology I generally try to avoid, heads are being thrust increasingly into boundary-spanning roles that differentiate them more and more from the teachers working on the core operations of the school.

I can well understand their dilemma. I still feel, however, that the answer has to be increased delegation of managerial responsibilities to others so that a teaching role, however small, can be maintained by the head. Otherwise it's all too easy for heads to lose sight of what they are managing *for*. They will certainly lay themselves open to charges from their staff that, in concentrating on relations with people outside the school, they have lost touch with its core function, which is to educate the young. Again, people's perceptions do matter.

Another buzz word from business management is 'empowerment', but teachers have always been empowered to take professional decisions in their own classrooms. One of the real joys of teaching has always been that the newest recruit to the staff has had considerable autonomy in this respect from day one. In the best run schools, teachers also played a full part in the consultative process leading up to decision making at the strategic management level for the school as a whole (it is a

25

definite plus for the managerial skills on display at Sidney Stringer that the young Estelle Morris so overtly feels herself to be part of the school's decision making processes in her probationary year). Thus, many of the better managed large secondary schools, where collegial discussion could not be taken for granted (as it largely was in the smaller primary schools), always had representative democracy built into their committee structures, etc.

There has also been a genuine exchange of ideas in these schools between the central and department/faculty levels that have been the only true layers of curricular management in most secondary schools. Thus there has not been the urgent need for delayering that the business sector has been forced to undertake to reduce hierarchical levels in recent years.

Learning organisations

The best managed schools have always been the learning organisations now so much advocated by the gurus of business management. They were establishments where the staff *were* regarded as creative, flexible and adaptive workers who were only too willing to share ideas in an open climate of discussion. Their teachers were not viewed as a sullen and devious workforce determined to resist change at all costs. Viewing employees as the latter, unfortunately, appears to have been an all too prevalent managerial attitude in parts of industry in the UK.

Consequently, it was generally accepted that having elaborate rule books of control backed up by draconian sanctions of the negative kind was not the best way to manage teachers. A much more effective strategy was to invest a large amount of trust in their capacity to work to the best of their abilities for the good of their pupils. Not all teachers, of course, lived up to these ideals, and control mechanisms had to be there for those who did not, but that was a court of last resort.

So why didn't industry pay more attention over the years to the managerial practices prevalent in education? Why weren't education managers called upon to lecture to their industrial counterparts about some of these vital principles? After all, these very same principles are now being imported via American business management gurus who are paid stratospheric sums of money per hour!

And why is it now being assumed that business management practices should be imported willy-nilly into education on the grounds that they are bound to improve the quality of pupils' learning? I think that's the raw material for another article about the rift between education and business and the relative status currently accorded to each of them in this country.

Have consultancy, will travel

Management consultants have a pretty bad name in educational circles. Most headteachers appear to put them above drug peddlers, journalists and gun runners in the occupational hierarchy but not a long way above. Indeed, most heads of my acquaintance hardly appear to view consultancy as a proper job at all. This view has certainly been encouraged by politicians of a certain tendency. When one Conservative minister was doing his education road shows, part of his knockabout humour was an anecdote about a talented talking tomcat named Fred, which was always coming home in the early mornings much the worse for wear after nights out on the tiles with his 'lady friends'. The annoyed owner had the animal neutered to make Fred less worn out during the days at home. Nevertheless, Fred's hectic night life seemed scarcely diminished after the operation, so the irritated owner asked him what he thought he was up to in his castrated state. "Oh, I'm a consultant now" replied Fred.

The odd thing about this kind of view being promulgated by politicians is obvious for all to see in the shape of those sections of the Nolan Committee Report on MPs' interests, and the subsequent, but no doubt totally coincidental, rush of Gadarene swine away from the House of Commons as declaration of the details of outside consultancies became obligatory. It's also noteworthy that some of the very headteachers who laughed so uproariously at this kind of jolly banter have since gone on to self-employment as management consultants. Nevertheless, despite pointing to some of the eternal inconsistencies of the human condition, I do wish to make a case for the increased use of management consultants in schools, and for the proposition that some of them might even be outsiders to the teaching profession.

I am well aware that this latter stance in particular is unlikely to put me high in the popularity stakes with school staff and I would like to speculate why this might be. There is an inclination on the part of heads and teachers to think that only those who work in schools on a regular basis can begin to understand how they should be managed. This attitude, while not unknown elsewhere, is not the prevalent one in a wide range of other organisations. It is often precisely because the management consultant has *not* spent his or her life involved in the manufacture of the particular kinds of widgets to which this or that firm has apparently been dedicated since the nineteenth century that the perspective which he or she brings to bear on the firm is so valued. Often, the consultant brings an invaluable reminder, to those who have long forgotten the original message, that the real purpose of the firm is to meet a particular need which has been met so far by the production of this kind of widget but which might well tomorrow, or even today, be better met by the production of a totally different kind of widget. (Someone should have told the majority of the manufacturers of clogs in the North of England that they were actually in the footwear business. Equally, I feel at times that schools should be reminded that they are in the pupil/learning, as opposed to the staff/teaching, business.)

Outsiders

In some cases it is better if the consultant in question has never been involved in the manufacture of widgets at all. This is not the same thing as saying that management consultants should have been consultants all their working lives. They certainly need to have actually had hands on managerial experience in some sphere or other in a previous occupational life. Nor is this an argument for consultants becoming permanent managers of the organisations that called them in in the first place. It is, however, so much easier for the outside observer to spot the obvious anomaly or anachronism than it is for the insider who has always accepted that 'this is the way things are organised around here'. In the chapter 'Rules to make you spit' in my earlier book *The Headteacher from Hell and Other Animals* (Questions Publishing 1996), I gave a series of examples where rules long past their sell-by date had been hung on to out of deeply ingrained habit rather than any kind of rational analysis. It is almost always the 'stranger' to the situation who asks the pertinent questions.

Consultants who are strangers to the organisations to which they are invited are usually careful to admit their initial ignorance and to avoid unwittingly telling their grandmothers how to suck eggs, at least in the early days of their consultancy. Yet there are still some management consultants from outside the world of education who too often do not recognise the depths of their own ignorance about schools. "After all", these consultants seem to conclude, "we have all been to schools ourselves for a considerable period of our lives. We are, therefore, in our own eyes at least, already knowledgeable about the work of our clients even before the consultancy begins". This leads to an over-reliance on the kind of in-built prejudice with which most of us are familiar in the saloon bar of our local hostelry. Everyone there is an expert on education based on his or her hazy recollections of their own days as school pupils in the increasingly far distant past. Not surprisingly, this kind of attitude does not endear such consultants to headteachers or their staffs.

Many heads would, however, be only too willing to concede how much they and their schools have gained from at least one other head being involved in their own appraisal since the new appraisal system came into being. Some of the most helpful of these appraising heads have been those who have treated the exercise very much as a management consultancy. They have been helped in this stance if the heads they are appraising have deliberately chosen areas of focus for the appraisal which they have recognised as potential weaknesses in their own managerial profile.

Mini-Ofsteds

Many LEAs have been understandably but unfortunately anxious not to make the appraisal process bear any resemblance, however faint, to a kind of mini-Ofsted inspection. They have given heads considerable latitude in a number of respects, including the choice of their own areas of focus in many cases. This has made it all too easy for heads who felt threatened by the whole notion of appraisal of their managerial performance to choose areas of focus where they felt personally and organisationally strong.

Where heads have, however, positively welcomed a probing of potential areas of weakness, the advice of other heads has been recognised as invaluable. This is very like the normal client-consultant relationship where a consultant is invited into the organisation to investigate ways of tackling what are usually seen as problems by the client (an invitation to review an organisation against a totally, or even relatively, open-ended brief seems to be a much rarer occurrence). The experienced consultant may not, of course, accept the clients' definitions of the problems; nevertheless, the starting point is a perceived deficiency on the part of the client, and certainly not a perceived strength! (I am deliberately discounting situations where the consultant is brought in to give an objective gloss to a solution to an organisational problem which the client already has firmly in mind, but would prefer someone outside the organisation to recommend. This is quite simply a prostitution of consultancy: the consultant as fall guy or hatchet woman.)

The most obvious advisers a school could turn to in the past were those officers often given that very title by many LEAs, but their role was never a true management consultancy role for more than one reason. First, at least in the secondary sector, their expertise was usually sharply delineated into curricular areas. Indeed, very few LEA secondary advisers have ever been headteachers or have had equivalent managerial experience; to go from being a secondary headteacher to being an adviser would usually involve the kind of drop in salary which few heads would ever contemplate. For these reasons, the 'expert consultancy' offered by secondary advisers was usually only as far up the school hierarchy as head of department level. This was even more the case with 'advisory teachers', who were usually appointed at lower salary levels than advisers.

Secondly, their relationship with the schools was double-edged, as they could be called upon from time to time to take an inspectorial line. Indeed, the terminology for the job veered between adviser and inspector, both between and (over periods of time) within LEAs. No organisation is willingly going to reveal weaknesses to a consultant who might later return, wearing a different hat, as an inspector with significant negative sanctions up his or her sleeve.

It is interesting to note that since advisers have been 'encouraged' to train as Ofsted inspectors, and since some LEAs have established their own Ofsted teams, the inspection work they do is usually only *outside* their own LEA. At least those schools who now view Ofsted teams as 'hit squads' know that their own advisers/inspectors will only be taking out contracts in some other neck of the woods.

Endangered species

Advisers, and advisory teachers even more so, are in any case rapidly becoming an endangered species in some LEAs as central government imposes ever tighter financial constraints on LEAs' education budgets. By the late 1970s the number of advisers had reached a high point of around 2,000 nationally, and the incoming government of 1979 soon began to talk in terms of LEA job creation schemes for what ministers publicly called 'the suede shoe brigade'. (Heaven knows how they labelled advisers in their more private utterances – perhaps along the same lines as former Prime Minister John Major labelled the Euro-sceptics when he thought the tape recorder had been switched off.) The national survey for 1992 to 1995 reported a continuing fall to 1,368 inspector/adviser posts, and there has been a much greater decline in advisory teacher posts: eight LEAs report that they now have no remaining posts of this kind at all. In addition, the remaining advisers are now often charged with being as self-financing as possible, which means they are preoccupied with, for example, the kind of Ofsted work already referred to.

So it looks as if heads will increasingly have to look elsewhere than their own LEA services for the kinds of consultancy they may need. They could, of course, turn to the growing army of ex-heads, ex-CEOs and ex-educationalists in general who appear only too willing to sell their services as consultants. These services often come relatively cheap in consultancy terms, because the individuals concerned are usually supplementing a pension rather than relying entirely on the consultancy fees for a living. The problem here is that one has to wonder why X retired from active service in the educational trenches at the remarkably early age of 42, or why Z has a suspicious entry in her CV from 1989 to 1992. It doesn't after all actually state that she was 'working as a consultant' in Holloway during those years.

So maybe there *is* an incentive to go outside the school world for consultancy after all. We had a striking example of the potential of outside consultancy in schools in the *Trouble-shooter* series on TV when Sir John Harvey-Jones gave glimpses of the remarkable transformation which had occurred in one school where he had been acting as a consultant for some years. Even allowing for the element of self-publicity involved, there did appear to be significant evidence of turn-round based at least in part on the advice proffered by Sir John. Perhaps other heads, either individually or in consortia, should be willing to consider the employment of experienced management consultants?

Taking the theses

JUDGING from the increase in the numbers of Masters and Doctoral applications we and other higher education institutions are receiving from managers in education these days, there is obviously a lot of interest in researching into aspects of education management. In this chapter I'm going to concentrate on the dissertation or thesis aspect of those degrees. Even taught courses almost always contain a dissertation element these days, and with research degrees (such as MPhil or PhD) the thesis is the key component.

I'm going to start with a modern Romanian fairy tale. I assure you there is considerable relevance to my main point, so please stick with it even if you're not into the kind of fairy stories promulgated by the Brothers Grimm etc. (I write this on the assumption that all managers have to be into the other kind of fairy tale from time to time if only to survive.)

The invincible rabbit

In the heart of one of the great Transylvanian forests there is a clearing with a little one-room cottage. In front of this abode, on a sunny summer's morning, a rabbit is sitting at a bench-like table thumping away at a word processor (I told you this was a fairy tale!). Into the clearing comes a fox. The fox sees the rabbit, comes closer and says: "So what are you up to then?"

"I'm writing up my PhD thesis," says the rabbit.

"Oh yeah," says the fox, in a somewhat sceptical tone of voice. "So what's it all about then?"

"The subject of my thesis is how rabbits kill and eat foxes, wolves and bears," replies the rabbit.

"I've never heard such a load of rubbish!" . . . is a polite version of the fox's response.

"You think so?" says the rabbit. "OK, come into my little house with me and I'll show you."

"Got him now," thinks the fox, and lopes across the rest of the clearing and into the house. There is the noise of a slight scuffle and then the rabbit reappears, cracking his finger joints prior to starting up again on the old word processor.

As told by Romanian academics on a festive evening when the good Murfatlar wine is flowing fast, this story can go on for a very, very long time. To cut it short, more or less the same dialogue goes on with a wolf and then a bear; the only significant difference is that each time the noise inside the cottage grows in proportion to the size of the animal entering the premises. But the outcome in every case is the same – the rabbit seems invincible.

So what's going on inside this cottage? OK, then, let's take a look inside. In the one corner of the room there is a pile of fox bones. In the second corner there is a pile of wolf bones. In the third corner there is a heap of bones from the late bear. And in the fourth corner, there is a very large and very well fed lion, a little bit the worse for wear from his encounters, but now snoozing very comfortably.

So what is the moral of this story? The moral is that it doesn't matter what you write about for your PhD. The thing that matters is who supervises it!

Reins of power

In Romania, under the benighted regime of the late and very unlamented dictator Ceausescu, this apparently was uncomfortably close to the literal truth. A small group of privileged and, as far as the ruling politicians were concerned, trusty professors in each subject field were widely acknowledged to hold the reins of power of the national approval system for PhDs. If one of them was your supervisor you were almost bound to be OK at the point of submission of the thesis.

However, the situation may be a good deal more complex for the UK student embarking upon a research degree. Plumping for one of the great and the good in the groves of academe as a research supervisor can certainly have its pay-off in terms of subsequent job applications. No country is without its academic glitterati, and hitching one's wagon to certain stars may be the fast track along the Milky Way. But there can be a downside to this. One world famous UK academic had his name taken in vain in the following piece of intramural university graffiti:

'What is the difference between Professor X and God? – God is everywhere. Professor X is everywhere but here!'

For there is a certain kind of globetrotting academic, perhaps best immortalised in the novels of David Lodge, who is definitely not a good bet as a supervisor if you are actually looking for advice on how next to proceed with your research. There may be very long gaps indeed between your delivery of sections of your work and your receipt of written comment, and that written comment may be short and often unsupported by face to face tutorials. The Professor Morris Zapps of this world are hard enough to contact by phone, fax or email, but actually expecting to see them in the flesh is really asking for too much.

Even those who have only national, as opposed to international, academic stardom can be difficult to pin down. The Germans have an expression – *D-Zug Professoren* or 'express train professors' – to cover those profs who seem to be in perpetual motion from one university to another in the *Bundesrepublik*. They deliver star turns on one night stands throughout the Fatherland, but are rarely available to see anyone in the university in which they are allegedly based. This situation has deteriorated even further since the fall of the Berlin Wall. Former West German academics have been actively encouraged by the reunified government to do 'missionary work' in the universities of the

new *Länder* to substitute for those former incumbents who were considered to be tainted by the previously dominant Marxist ideology.

Publishing practicalities

There is also the problem that, although some of the academic 'names' may hardly deign to see you during your time as a research student under their nominal tutelage, they may suddenly become much more interested in your research if it appears to be in any way publishable. The snag is that their advice on getting your work published may just involve the attachment of their names to the submission for publication. From your point of view, unfortunately, there may be more than a grain of practical sense in this approach, as the great and the good who edit the 'learned journals' have a habit of recognising their own when it comes to accepting papers for publication. But if you feel obliged to go along with this dubious strategy for the sake of your future career, beware the 'offer' of your supervisor to put his or her name first when it comes to the joint authorship. It may be suggested to you that it doesn't really matter whether your name comes first or second but, believe me, it does matter a very great deal under the arcane rules of the academic game. The first named author is the kingpin. You might even end up as a mere '*et al*', anonymously trailing behind your 'benefactor' when other great and the good later cite the work in question.

What you really need is to serve an apprenticeship, not with one of the chief academic sorcerers in the land, but with a supervisor who has the time, knowledge, understanding and inclination to help others come to terms with the often arduous process of research. While researching undoubtedly has its highs when you feel you really have had deep and original insights into a topic which fascinates you, there are also the lows. You can become periodically convinced that these very same 'insights' are really only blinding glimpses of the obvious. Or, any number of things can appear to be going wrong simultaneously, and you really do have to have that 'stickability' factor that will take you through to completion.

There is a (no doubt apocryphal) tale in the groves of academe familiar to me of a tutor who has had any number of research students to supervise over a great many years but has yet to have a single one of his protégés achieve a successful completion. Now we have to accept that the main cause of 'failure' at the PhD level is drop-out before completion, but surely not all this tutor's students are congenitally lacking in persistence?

Genuine interest

This is why it's important to choose a subject for your research which holds genuine long-term interest and usefulness for you and your school, as opposed to merely 'taking one off the peg'. Your supervisor may direct you to a topic only because he or she is out to add another layer to the research structure currently in vogue at the University of X. The other danger with many a currently fashionable research topic is that it may be 'a blaze in the stubble after which all is darkness', to paraphrase Cardinal Newman.

Theses take a long time to complete, particularly if you're working on them part time, as most managers in education are now that the days of secondments are long gone. It's no use at all to your career advancement if your topic was the flavour of the month some four years or so ago but is now merely regarded as a flash in the pan. Fortunately, many of the issues of education management remain permanently fascinating as areas of research because they are, in the end, concerned with that most intriguing of subjects – humanity in all its infinite variety. And don't ever forget (though at times you may be tempted to) that supervisors are a part of that very same varied humanity.

Ofsted: the aftermath

Most of us in education have by now seen all too many examples of Ofsted reports. Some of us also have growing collections of the letters which chairs of governing bodies feel they have to add to the summary of the report which they are obliged to send out to the parents of the school's pupils. It seems unfair to mock the afflicted, but I now present a totally fictitious example of the kind of letter which many a misguided governing body might feel tempted to write following an underwhelming vote of approval by the Ofsted inspectors. Of course, the latter might themselves be equally misguided, but in rather different ways.

10 September 1997

Dear Parents,

The governing body have enclosed the summary of the Ofsted report dating back to our inspection of July 1997.

We are conscious of the many strengths which the inspection team recorded amongst their findings but we are concerned that these positive conclusions might be overlooked when the report is made available to the press on 11 September. It is only too well known that the press likes nothing better than to sensationalise criticism of schools, and it is unfortunately true that there are aspects of the report which could provide ammunition to the more unscrupulous amongst the journalistic profession. In the following gloss on the report, we hope, therefore, to give a more balanced perspective than parents might gain from press reports alone.

It is sadly true that at the time of the inspection our former headteacher, Mrs Jones, was on protracted sick leave, and you will be aware that she took early retirement on the grounds of ill-health over the August period. It is also our sad duty to report that the acting head at the time of the inspection, the then deputy, Mr Johnson, has followed her into retirement. The governors acted swiftly by appointing Mr Graveman as acting head immediately after the inspection. He is on a temporary secondment from St Luke's Infant and Junior School in the west of the Borough. We regret that he has already informed us that he will not be applying for the substantive post when it is advertised this term, but we have little doubt that we will attract a good field of forward-looking managers at the competitive salary we are able to offer.

This somewhat difficult and turbulent period in the management of the school no doubt helps to account for the inspectors having perceived that there appeared to be an ethos of 'blind aimlessness' in the running of the school. While feeling that this judgement might be somewhat 'over the top', particularly if it is quoted out of context, we do have to admit with hindsight that the absence of a written school development plan was a mistake in this bureaucratic age in which we all now live. The governing body is convinced that its close-knit teamworking and consensus-seeking style of decision making had led to a situation in which our aims for the school were so well known and generally accepted that to formalise them on paper would have been an unnecessary afterthought. That is, however, not the way the pettifogging bureaucrat apparently sees things.

We have no right of appeal against the rather harsh statement of the Registered Inspector, which has predictably been subsequently rubber-stamped by Her Majesty's Chief Inspector, that the school was failing to give its pupils an acceptable standard of education. That this judgement is in stark contradiction to the overall evaluation by you and your fellow parents, as recorded in the responses to the questionnaire which we distributed to you at the time of the inspection, apparently carries no weight at all with the 'powers that be'.

You will recall that there was an overwhelmingly positive response to such questions as: 'I feel that the school is giving my child an excellent education' (91% strongly agreeing or agreeing) and 'I am perfectly satisfied with the school's governing body' (93% strongly agreeing or agreeing), etc. To cast doubt now on this outstanding endorsement, by nit-picking about the ways in which the questionnaires were distributed, collected and collated, seems deplorably typical of the jumped-up jackboots mentality of what amounted more to a hit squad than a genuine inspection team.

The comments on staff morale seem equally misplaced and would be quite likely to damage the school's image and reputation if they were reported to the wider public in a distorted fashion. We accept that it was unfortunate that six members of staff resigned in the term in which the inspection took place, but we are confident that the 'demoralisation' referred to in the report was for the most part a result of the inspection itself. It is hard to think of anything more demoralising than the prospect of having your teaching judged 'less than satisfactory' by a bunch of part-time amateurs who looked as though they had never been in a classroom in their lives. To refer to exceptional levels of staff absence and illness as a barometer of staff morale is typical of the crude yardsticks adopted by the Inspectorate.

Equally, we are not best pleased by some of the comments about the pupil behaviour made by the inspectors. It seems to us to be praising with faint damns to write that: 'Generally pupils know right from wrong'. Would that we were so confident of the inspectors' ability to make such a distinction! The fact that we had excluded 43 pupils during the year ought surely to have been seen as a testimony to our commitment to high achievement and standards rather than the opposite. We have adopted a widely-praised policy of 'zero tolerance' towards disruptive pupil behaviour, and the regrettable classroom incidents referred to in the inspection report no doubt reflect the not altogether inaccurate perception on the part of a few pupils that they were 'untouchable' during the period of the inspection itself. To blame these flagrant attempts at attention seeking on the fact that some classes had had more than seven teachers in the course of the year seems to us to be a blatant example of the inspectors' inability to distinguish cause from effect.

It is interesting to note that the inspectors could not deny that the standards in design and technology at Key Stage 2 were above the national average, and that in both key stages the standards in music and geography were similar to those found in most schools. It is important to point out these significant successes because the report itself does not in general tend to underline the plus points. Indeed, the report seems to us unduly negative about results which might easily be very different this time next year. If we adopted a similar policy about announcing school sports results in assembly, we would hardly raise the spirits of the pupils in the way which our present policy of only announcing the wins does. It has always been our policy to accentuate the positive.

It is, therefore, against our own better judgement that we are obliged by law to inform parents that we are now in what are called 'special measures'. We have to draw up an ACTION PLAN (following the somewhat odd use of capital letters in the inspection report itself) within 40 working days of receiving the report, showing what the school is going to do about the issues identified by the inspectors. This plan will be circulated to all parents at the school. We are confident that this letter has demonstrated that your school's governing body will be well able to show how the school can continue to go from strength to strength.

Signed on behalf of the governing body by Joe Bloggs.

Author's note: I happen to have a copy of this letter on which someone has scrawled the following comments in green ink:

"Some hopes! But at least this lot didn't whinge on about 'the social context of the school'. If I have to read yet again about 'mitigating circumstances' such as the below national average level of good housing and the relatively poor prospects of employment; the above national average level of families with English as a second language; the astronomically high uptake of free school meals; the 'creaming off' of bright pupils by other schools in the area; etc. etc, I'll throw up."

There is evidence that this was written by somebody connected with Ofsted. I did state at the outset that maybe it wasn't just the governors who were misguided.

The secretary from hell

IN MY last collection, *The Headteacher from Hell*, referred to earlier, I included an article which dealt with the issue of how to misuse and abuse the school secretary – in the fervent, but no doubt misguided, hope that some guilty parties would see the error of their ways. There is, however, a reverse side to the coin. The first school in which I taught was, to a very real extent, under the domination of the school secretary, a Scottish lady of formidable countenance and demeanour. The head was completely under her thumb and the staff lived in mortal fear of her. Indeed, there were those on the staff who reckoned that the site map issued to visitors ought to have had a warning arrow pointing to the secretary's office with the message: *Here be ye dragon.*

Her whole existence could have been written up as a case study in how to wield power and influence from a position not normally seen as one of total authority. Every year, for example, she would take a day's annual leave on the Friday before FA Cup Final day so she could travel down to London in style and comfort to see her one soccer match of the year. She had, of course, a seat in the stands on the great day itself, something which the men on the staff (and this was an all-boys grammar school) would have given an arm and a leg for. She let it be known that this was an annual privilege for which she did not pay one farthing, and dropped heavy hints to the effect that this was a gift from a known but anonymous benefactor. The general view in the staff room was that the then President of the Football Association was being blackmailed by her in much the same way as was the head, who clearly dared not cross her on even the most trivial aspect of school protocol.

The one advantage of her dominating presence in the school from the staff's point of view was that, if you had any troublesome teenager who was not responding to your own persuasive charms, you could threaten the aforementioned troublemaker with being sent to the school secretary. This usually produced cowed submission for the rest of the lesson at least. Nobody dreamed of sending pupils to the head, which would have been regarded by the pupils as a doddle by comparison.

This was one version of the secretary from hell, but I have in mind today a couple of other variations on the theme which are built on somewhat different lines. I apologise for any inferred sexism in the following, but we might as well accept the present reality that it's nearly always 'she' as far as school secretaries are concerned. I should, however, make it clear that I have met and worked with some excellent females in this role to contrast with the pair of hell-hags I am now going to depict.

The serial slacker

Let's take the idle, incompetent and downright slovenly model for starters. Her basic precepts would appear to be as follows:

- If anyone rings, let the telephone go on ringing until you've finished reading the article in 'Hello' magazine which is your current preoccupation (this assumes you are actually present when the phone rings; make no provision whatsoever for those occasions when you are not in the office).

- If and when you pick up the phone, make it clear from your tone that you are not best pleased at being disturbed. A peremptory

"Yes?!" expressed with the correct degree of exasperation is enough to set the conversation rolling merrily along.

• If pressed as to who you are, give your name only. Do not tell the caller the name of the school as well, but keep them guessing as to whether or not they've dialled the Chinese takeaway in error. On no account announce yourself as the school secretary. It's no business of theirs what your job is.

• If anyone rings for the head, just put the caller straight through. Don't bother to check the name or the purpose of the call, or whether the head's tied up with other matters.

• If the person being called isn't available, just say so. Teachers are in the school to teach, not receive phone calls, so by definition no teacher is available. Don't offer to take a message – you're not

47

running a telegram service.

• If callers insist on leaving a message, tell them to wait while you find a pen and a notepad. You will probably find that if you spin this out long enough they won't be on the end of the line when you eventually get back to them. Some people have no patience! If, by any unfortunate chance, they *are* still on the line and showing signs of impatience, start to take the message, muttering, "I've only got one pair of hands, you know." Interrupt almost immediately to the effect that you don't do shorthand and tell them to slow down. If they look like going on for more than a minute or so, point out that you have other more important things to do and suggest they might like to write.

• Don't take the caller's name, address or telephone number. If they omit to give you these details, that's their lookout. It should make the recipient of the message intrigued to find out who was calling.

• If any callers are looking for further information, a good response is: "Don't ask me, I only work here." They're very unlikely to bother you further because they will have instantly got the message that you're an oppressed helot who is deliberately kept in the dark by 'management'.

• If the telephone callers are after the head or the deputies who *might* just be available, you will have to make the effort to determine whether the latter are in their offices. If the top brass don't answer when you try to connect them, tell the caller you haven't a clue where they are, and ask them to call back later. If the caller persists that some representative of the senior management *must* be available to take the call, imply that as of now *you* are that representative and that this is quite a common occurrence.

• If a couple of parents should call in person, irately demanding to see the head and looking as though they want instant revenge, send them straight in. This is not your fight, but you will surely enjoy the noises emanating from the next room during the following half hour. Should the head later query why you let them loose, say that you did your level best to head them off at the pass but they just pushed their way past you.

• It's important to have excuses ready to cover up any of your mistakes which are latched on to. Indeed, never admit to *any* mistakes, even if you know they're going to really blow up sooner or later. By that time you might have been able to cover your own tracks, and that's far more important than saving the head from getting egg all over his or her face.

Malice in Blunderland

Far worse than the slattern from the head's point of view is the deviously malicious secretary, whose precepts appear to run along the following lines:

• It's only human nature that you'll have favourites among the members of staff. Make no attempt to disguise this with them. Indeed, it's the whole purpose of preferential treatment to show who's in and who's out currently. For those who are not the flavour of the month, you can make access to the head almost impossible. The head's diary will always be full at just the times they want an audience.

• For your bugbears on the staff, always be on the lookout for any touch of the old acid you can drop into the head's ear about them. Paranoia is an occupational disease of all heads, so feed it on every occasion possible. Implying to the head that you suspect Miss James is not 100% loyal to the school is almost bound to be an accurate statement of fact in any case. It isn't your fault that the head overreacted so badly.

• There are, however, a thousand subtle ways in which you can rubbish, marginalise and demonise those on the staff you dislike without having to resort to such open calumny as the above. If Mr Johnson scribbles you a hurried note under intense pressure

49

asking to see the head, and it contains a spelling error, make sure the evidence in question goes through to the head in all its original offending glory. If you think the head's going to be possibly too busy (or even too illiterate) to spot the mistake, a subtle touch of the old red biro should draw the requisite attention. If you've already seduced the head into a joint conspiracy of contempt for the 'idiots' on the staff, you can cheerfully draw large rings of red biro round such inaccuracies. This will also demonstrate your desire to maintain the high standards of the school which some of these recent recruits to what is laughingly called the teaching profession are in danger of bringing into disrepute. You are only too well aware that you are more intelligent than they are, and if you had not been unfairly held back by your home, your social class, your deprivation etc, then your natural superiority to them would have received the public recognition it so clearly deserves.

• You can convey a lot to the head about your opinions of members of staff without any use of words at all. Just look to the heavens for assistance every time the head mentions Jane Saunders, and the goose of Jane's reputation as an efficient organiser is going to be well and truly cooked. Jim Fleming's name on the head's lips and an accompanying roll of the eyes on your part will be enough to ensure that young Jim had better seek promotion elsewhere.

• Unlike the slattern, you will not push the mail through to the head unsorted and unprioritised. Why throw up the wonderful opportunity not only to control, but to a large extent direct, the information flow? The odd scribbled 'dealt with' can cover a multitude of sins. Information is power and nobody, but nobody, is going to be more informed than you in this outfit. Even the odd letter marked 'private and confidential', but with an intriguing postmark or envelope, can be opened on the pretext that you had so many letters to deal with this morning you just didn't notice (you don't have the necessary privacy for steaming them open).

• At the end of the day, all documents come back into your hands for filing in any case. That might be a chore to some, but to you it's a labour of love (and hate). As you weigh up your decisions to file and misfile according to your whim, you can revel in the power you wield so capriciously. Your only regret is that few on the staff will ever realise how much their fate was in your hands throughout the whole of their 'careers'.

Dear Agony Aunt . . .

I ALWAYS felt that what *Managing Schools Today* was missing was an agony column where heads and others could seek advice on their current issues of pressing concern. So (as reproduced in this and the next two chapters) I procured the services of a hard-boiled agony aunt, 'Hard-hearted Hannah' to give the magazine's readers some examples (totally fictitious, of course) of problems and advice in tune with the often brutal realities of our time.

Interfering governors

I am the head of an LEA primary school in what has become the 'Hampstead' or 'Greenwich Village' area of the city in which we live. The effect of this is that my governing body largely consists of what I understand are referred to these days as 'Champagne Socialists', who are constantly interfering with my management of the school. This recently came to a head when they insisted on my removing from the school prospectus any reference to the fact that our success rate for pupils entering the nearest grant maintained secondary grammar school is second to none in the city. They claim that this showed my 'obsession with examination success' and that this should be a school where 'all-round personal development' was the more important aim. Some of these governors are prominent local politicians. What can I do?

There is a simple solution to your problem. Hint that the local rag has contacted you with a view to running a series of features on governors of LEA schools who have sent their own children to this GM grammar school (you will almost certainly be aware that many of your trendy lefty governors who have older children will fall into this category, which explains their embarrassment at your proposed prospectus entry). Imply that you think this is a gross intrusion of privacy that you would not want to encourage. Nevertheless, it would make it clear that your school sees no reason to apologise for its record in this respect if the pupils' success rate for entry into the GM grammar school were featured prominently in the school prospectus. If they still cavil, underline the need for mutual cooperation in situations such as these. They will soon get the message.

Religious foibles

I am the head of a heavily oversubscribed C of E school in a part of the inner city which has a relatively high Muslim population. I suspect that many of the parents who wish to send their children to the school are only doing so because the local mosques discourage their own worshippers from sending their children to us. This means that some people see us as a 'White Highlands School', which is attractive to them for what I regard as precisely the wrong reasons. I would wish our school to reflect in its pupils the rich multicultural mix of what used to be our local catchment area.

Discard these namby-pamby notions forthwith and join the real world. It won't be long before the Government accepts the inevitable logic of allowing Muslims the same rights for schools as the Church of England and all the other religions already under the net (note the prescience here of our agony aunt – D.E.H.). So you can forget these empty-headed dreams of inter-faith schooling.

Capitalise instead on your marketing possibilities. Do a deal with the local vicars and run a points system for entry to the school linked to parental attendance at church services. If parents realise they have to go to church to get their children into your school, church attendance will boom as never before. Who can then argue we're a secular society? Ask for a percentage of the church collections as a quid pro quo. *This will boost your school funds no end.*

Pass the buck

The one selective grant maintained secondary school in our area celebrated its first year after the departure from LEA control by, amongst other things, heading the national league table for permanent exclusions of disruptive pupils. The poor old LEA then found its referral units full to the gunwales, and there was irresistible pressure to increase the number of these units despite their disproportionate expense to run. The financial limit for that increase has now been reached. The school did not, however, apparently relish the media publicity it received from topping the expulsions league, and has now changed its tactics in such a way that the pressure is now not on the referral units but on schools such as the one I head.

In brief, their pupils are no longer excluded. They now leave voluntarily! The trick seems to be to 'invite' to the school the parents of identified troublemakers or even just your common or garden 'underachievers', then persuade them that it would be in the best interests of their offspring to transfer them to friendly neighbourhood LEA comprehensives such as our own.

The official line is that the parents are informed that the rigorously academic approach of the GM school is driving these sensitive youngsters to desperation, whereas what they *need* is the warm, cuddly approach of the local comps. I suspect the unofficial line is to give parents the choice between voluntary transfer of this kind and the threat of involuntary despatch to the local 'sin bins'. Given the reputation of the 'hulks', as they have been known since their overcrowding in recent times, this is an offer the parents can hardly refuse. Hence our current problems as we are 'chosen' time and time again for transfers of this kind.

Some of my staff are typifying my acceptance of such pupils as evidence of my liberal do-gooding, but as far as I can see I have little choice in the matter. To re-exclude such children would be tantamount to giving up on them, given the present constraints on LEA spending on extra places in referral units. This would ultimately present the community with massive long-term problems. Yet I fear a staff mutiny if this present situation continues. What can I do?

What colour is the sky on your planet? The name of this game is 'pass the parcel'. Pupils excluded once are prime targets for further exclusions. The fact that you haven't referred to your school's governors suggests that they are not themselves of the 'no exclusions under any circumstances' brigade – so, there must be some other school at the end of the line who will be the ones found to be holding all the parcels once the music stops. You will know when the music stops because that's when the Secretary of State will send in the Ofsted hit squad. It will also be the time when the senior management team will be pilloried by the press for 'lack of leadership in failing to turn the school around'. Guess who will be first in line for the old heave-ho at that point? This is dog-eat-dog time in education so, unless you wish to be the sacrificial hot dog in your area, wise up and ship out the problem cases. After all, transportation of Britain's undesirables worked remarkably well until some of the colonies started getting ideas above their station. Remember that a 'sink school' today is a 'sunk school' tomorrow.

Save your own skin

Following a reduced intake this year to the girls' secondary school which I head, I insisted that all staff holding 'key positions' in the school should become actively involved in a recruitment programme. This was non-negotiably added to their job descriptions, and I made clear to them in no uncertain terms that we can't allow this under-recruitment to become a trend of falling rolls or their jobs are on the line. Subsequently, one of the local primary schools asked us to arrange an evening entertainment for them involving some of our star gymnasts. Two of our PE staff chose a group of five of our pupils, and together they put on what was certainly seen by the primary school head as a successful event which should definitely help our recruitment drive.

Unfortunately, the school minibus was out of action at the time, and the girls were asked to turn up at the primary school for 6pm. At the end of the evening, when it was dark, the two teachers involved drove three of the pupils to their homes in the one car they had available. The other two pupils who lived closer volunteered to travel home under their own steam. The chair of governors has now received a formal written complaint from the parents of these two girls to the effect that they were allowed to walk to the bus stop and travel home unaccompanied at considerable risk to themselves. What do I now do?

Presumably you were wise enough to put nothing in writing instructing the PE teachers to conduct the event (the job description extension shouldn't be a problem because this was not specifically a recruitment evening). If my assumption is correct, now's the time to ditch them. Loyalty is a one-way street these days. You can describe the event as a voluntary extra-curricular activity undertaken by two teachers who had clearly not followed all the correct school procedures. Again I assume, no doubt correctly, that you have a staff procedural handbook of such size and complexity that nobody could possibly follow all of its rules and regulations and do anything like a sensible and worthwhile job of work. Therefore, you will be right in thinking that nobody pays any attention to it until an incident of this kind arises. Now, however, it will be worth its weight in pieces of silver to you (30 of them to be precise).

Arrange a disciplinary hearing at which the governors will absolve you of all blame and give at least an oral warning to the two teachers concerned as to their future conduct. This may give you a few little local difficulties as far as getting 'volunteers' for future activities of this kind is concerned, but it's better to be safe than sorry when it's a matter of your own personal liability or that of the school that's at stake.

The agony continues . . .

D UE TO the tremendous success of the advice given in her first agony column, our agony aunt, 'Hard-hearted Hannah', from the new school of brutalism, continues in this chapter with a further crop of readers' problems.

Stoned again?

There has been an increasing problem of some of our pupils manifesting extreme mood swings consistent with their being on drugs or glue sniffing. I have tried to raise this with their parents, but with some I get little but verbal abuse in return. At best there is a general reluctance to accept that this could be a problem which relates to their children. The governing body of my school also appears oddly reluctant to discuss the issue. I am now considering taking the matter to the local constabulary or even writing an article in the local press about what I see a mounting threat to society. What would you advise?

Do you have a death wish? Do you imagine you're the only headteacher facing this problem? We know from all the surveys that this is indeed a widespread societal problem, particularly amongst the young. Do you imagine that Trainspotting *was a cult film with teenagers because the title misled them into imagining it was all about Thomas the Tank Engine, or because they admired the literary style of the novel?*

So why has there been such a devastating silence from the vast majority of the headteachers of the land about this issue? The answer's very simple. Admit just once that the problem exists in your school, and you and your staff are dead meat with a BSE certificate to match. As you have quite accurately discovered, parents don't want to know about this issue as far as their own offspring are concerned. Ostriches with heads in the sand have 20/20 vision compared to this lot when the 'D-word' is mentioned. If they want a conspiracy of silence, who are you to stir up trouble? Do you really want to set the national record for falling rolls? Read Ibsen's An Enemy of the People *or, if that's too literary for you, catch the next time the film* Jaws *comes up on TV and remind yourself what happens to the messenger who bears the bad news. Nobody, but nobody, wants to hear about this happening in their schools in their town.*

Compete or die

I am convinced that the politicians are correct when they urge us in schools to uphold the moral and spiritual values which have helped to provide the cohesion necessary for the very survival of our society. At the same time, our school is faced with increasing competition for pupils by neighbouring schools which are mounting campaigns of aggressive marketing aimed at the parents in our locality. I find it hard to regard education as a commercial business, but it seems as if we must either compete to 'win' at the expense of others, or run the risk of declining in numbers to the point where our very survival may be threatened. How do I resolve what I see as a growing ethical dilemma?

Welcome to the real world! Who do you think passed the laws which have set school against school and head against head? Who has turned pupils into age-weighted cash units? It wasn't the tooth fairy that was behind all this but the self-same politicians who blame teachers for not inculcating moral values in the young. Yes, you've got it, the very same politicians who take cash for questions and view the world from the summit of the sleaze mountain. A market model where each unit pursues its own interests and lets the devil take the hindmost is hardly likely to lead to the general good of all. In the economic market there are inevitably winners and losers, so which group do you want to line up with? In other words, put the dilemma firmly back where it belongs, which is at the feet of the politicians themselves – and while they're pontificating (which may be for some time yet, so don't hold your breath), you'd better compete or die.

Negative promotion

I am the head of a large co-educational secondary comprehensive school. In recent years many of the best teachers in the school have been promoted to positions of responsibility but have often quickly vacated them as they have sought and obtained even higher promotions in other schools. Now groups of parents are complaining of the high turnover of staff in the school and the consequent disruption of their children's schooling. How can I ensure a greater sense of long-term loyalty to the school on the part of the staff?

You really do need a few lessons in management technique, don't you? You've obviously been promoting people on merit. You'll get no gratitude from those you promote if they are well aware of their worth and clearly probably regard the promotion as overdue recognition of their obvious talents. For such staff, internal promotions are, as you have rightly observed, merely stepping stones on their road to advancement. No matter what dark hints you might drop, there is no way these men and women are going to regard leaving the school for employment elsewhere as a treasonable offence. Having taken this approach to internal promotions, you have almost certainly diminished your power over them because it would seem a trifle odd for you to give them lousy references when they then apply elsewhere. It might even be taken to imply that your judgement of their abilities was at fault when you promoted them.

The answer is obvious. You must only promote those who seem to their colleagues unworthy of promotion because they apparently lack the necessary leadership qualities. To the imperceptive observer this may appear to have certain disadvantages, but consider for a moment the many advantages. These people will be forever in your debt and will be only too well aware that nobody but you would have raised them on high. They will be determined to prove to themselves that you were right all along to spot their hitherto hidden potential, and they will probably rule their subordinates with a rod of iron because of their inner doubts as to their own capabilities. They will also now have the chance to settle old scores with the erstwhile colleagues who clearly held them in such low esteem.

However, they themselves are going nowhere. They will probably live in perpetual self-doubt as to whether they should ever have risen as high as they already have, never mind take on even greater and, to them, more daunting responsibilities elsewhere. Fear of failure will be a big enough ghost to constantly haunt them even at the present level to which you have (over-) promoted them. Furthermore, they will always deferentially welcome your guiding hand when it comes to their managerial responsibilities. They and their fragile egos will live in perpetual anxiety at the thought of any criticism you might level at their actions. This will permanently tie them to whatever is your current party line. These will not be potential robber barons who might be a threat to your regal authority, but loyal and subservient followers who will acknowledge their feudal oath of allegiance. They will be there to toast your good health when you eventually retire after very many years of dedication to your school – because it's quite clear from your question that you're not going anywhere either.

With fond memories . . .

A year ago I became the head of a medium-sized primary school of which I was previously the deputy head. I was determined that on taking up my new appointment I would not be cast in the same aloof mould as my predecessor, who, for example, was only to be seen in the staffroom on very rare occasions. I have gone out of my way to be as accessible to the rest of the staff as I was in my former deputy role. Recently, however, I have become more and more aware of a certain tension in the air when I am in the staffroom. Conversations noticeably stop short when I enter the room. I asked my deputy if I was imagining this and she reinforced my fears by telling me that the staff are beginning to talk about my predecessor in more and more favourable terms – as someone who is now apparently seen as having let them get on with their own business in the staffroom and was never 'snooping around'. These words hurt me, I have to admit, and I am beginning to wonder if I have adopted the wrong policy.

Too true you have! I have some very sound advice for you on this one. But first of all you will have to recognise that no matter what polices you pursue, as the years roll by your predecessor will inexorably grow in stature and fond memory in the minds of your staff. This is known in the trade as the 'Rebecca myth'. Last night your staff dreamed they went to Manderley again, and they remembered with fond nostalgia all the virtues which your predecessor possessed. While she was in post, of course, they cursed these very same virtues as the vices they then recognised so very acutely. But nothing you or anybody else can now say will make them accept to themselves or anyone else that they ever harboured such dark feelings about that blessed lady who grows more saintly with every passing day. The only crumb of comfort for you is that after you've left the school you will also probably become a legend in your own lifetime.

But let's get back to the here and now, where you are committing one of the unpardonable sins of headship. Go into the staffroom late one night (when there is no Ofsted inspection looming or just completed, and when everyone but you has left the building) and ask yourself what it reminds you of. The shabby surroundings covered with the detritus of years; chipped mugs with the remains of two day old coffee; dog-eared posters announcing long-gone events; the general air of studied untidiness, etc. etc. Yes, you've got it – it's just like the bedroom of your teenage son or daughter! What does this tell you? Right, this is the holy of holies, the sanctum sanctorum through the portals of which authority figures should only enter with express permission on very rare and special occasions.

Would you dream of entering your teenager's bedroom without knocking on the door first? You would? Well in that case, you're possibly irredeemable but, just for the record, heads are not wanted in staffrooms. These are places where staff want to sound off about all the ills of the world, which are bound to include some they see you as inflicting upon them. If they can't chunter on in the staffroom in peace, the pressure will build up until one day they explode in your face. So for goodness' sake, allow them their decompression chamber where they can share their tales of the battles of the day, safe in the knowledge that you are in your bunker planning the next campaign in which they will once again be the poor bloody infantry.

These are the unfortunate facts of a head's life. The staff have got to have somebody to blame and you're as well placed as most to fit that bill. Accept that fact, live with it, and maybe one day they (and maybe even your offspring) will have fond memories of you. If it could happen to the first Mrs de Winter, it could happen to anybody!

Piling on the agony

As THERE appears to be no shortage of heads seeking advice from our no nonsense agony aunt, here is a third selection of reader's queries and their shock-jock treatment by Hard-Hearted Hannah.

Wasted efforts

Our comprehensive school is having great difficulty in attempting to teach personal and social education (PSE) to Key Stage 4 pupils, who just do not seem to appreciate the efforts their teachers make to cover such vital elements as (for example) sex education or education for democratic citizenship. It is increasingly difficult to find teachers willing to take on such work, and there is an alarming degree of absenteeism among those teachers who have to be drafted in despite their protests. As some of these teachers are among the best in their own specialist subject areas, I feel the process is becoming self-defeating. What do you advise?

Get real! Accept that government words about the importance of such work are just that – words. Is PSE examinable in your school?

Of course it isn't. So what follows, as sure as night follows day? The pupils can easily recognise that any time devoted to such activity is taking them away from what they see as their major purpose in school at this stage – namely success in their GCSE examination subjects as a hoped-for passport to later career advancement. Furthermore, their teachers feel much the same, with the added wrinkle that they feel neither qualified nor trained to 'deliver' topics such as those you have identified.

The curriculum is overloaded as it is at this stage despite Ron Dearing's best efforts to slim it down. Would you feel confident that you could teach sex education under such circumstances without the occasional riot? As for 'democratic citizenship', to what extent is your school a genuinely democratic society? Do you have representational government of the school? Is there a school council on which pupils have representatives with a genuine say in the way the organisation operates? No? So why shouldn't pupils suspect the whole thing is a sham and prepare for an adult life in which they can feel as alienated from politics as an increasing percentage of the population appears to be?

As for sending some of your best subject teachers into this quagmire, this prompts the question: 'What does this area contribute to your league table position?' Zilch! That's what. So this is where you place those teachers who, through incompetence or their own ill-fortune, have gaps in their subject timetables. It should be clearly marked as a way station to the scrapheap. To change the metaphor, you are sending some troops over the top to walk across no-man's land (PSE, as it exists at present, is no-woman's land as well), as a clear warning to those still in the trenches that it could be their turn next if the right exam results aren't forthcoming.

The perils of pensions

I fear that the teachers' pensions arrangements announced by the last government will make it altogether too costly to allow teachers to retire in their fifties. The new and much more stringent conditions applied to breakdown pensions will also make it difficult for teachers to retire early on grounds of ill health. School managers like me are therefore going to be faced with some

ageing and disaffected teachers who will reduce the general level of quality of pupils' education. What can be done about this?

Don't despair. My answer to the previous question gives you some indications as to what to do with these staff. If the present over-cumbersome dismissal processes are not streamlined by law soon (and once again Hannah demonstrates her clairvoyant talents – D.E.H.), *more drastic action may be needed. There are already some very interesting private enterprise schemes springing up which may meet your needs. How about the contract killing agencies which allow you to target your public enemies for hit men and women to take out? (A service which has long been widely available in such places as Belfast and Palermo.)*

Involuntary euthanasia services are also on the way, but these should only be resorted to once you have exhausted the voluntary suicide channels. Announce each year the targets for staffing

65

reductions at which the school must aim, and ask for volunteers to make the ultimate sacrifice. Eulogise about the heroic self-sacrificing qualities of explorers such as Captain Oates during school assemblies. It shouldn't be long before some declining member of staff gets the message and goes out into the winter snows muttering "I may be gone for some time".

If this fails to work, hold staff meetings in which pointed remarks are made about the impossibility of carrying excess baggage in these turbulent times. Make it plain that unless some are cleared out of the way in a deliberate and planned way, it will all boil down to a lottery at the end of the year in which those who draw the short straws will take the rap. This should ensure that the number of fatalities amongst the staff will quickly increase: car brakes will fail, teachers will mysteriously fall from upstairs windows, etc. The beauty of this approach is that the staff will feel that they themselves have ownership of the solution. It will be a tribute to your team building qualities.

Downmarket blues

I am the deputy head of a primary school in one of the most deprived inner city areas of a large Northern industrial town. We have, for example, the highest proportion of pupils on free school meals of any school in the town. The parents of our pupils are what used to be described as solidly working class except that in our area most of them can't get jobs any more. Not surprisingly, we came very close to the bottom of the national primary school performance tables in the 1996 Key Stage 2 results. Do you think this is likely to adversely affect my chances of obtaining a headship in the kind of middle class suburban school where I would like to spend the last twenty years or so of my teaching career?

Too true it is! As the man said to the driver asking for instructions on how to get to his desired destination: "If I were you, I wouldn't start from here." Your mistake was to take an appointment in one of these outfits in the first place. Not many Harley Street doctors made their way there via a stint working as medics in leper colonies.

Former Education Minister Gillian Shephard was, of course, convinced that if you could do a spot of canvassing for the Conservative Party and persuade your local citizenry to vote Tory, your school would have immediately entered the Premier League, but then Scheherazade spun a good yarn about the similar properties of magic carpets. Leaving the fantasy league tables and re-entering the real world, I assume your staff have already tried teaching to the test, the whole test, and nothing but the test? If not, then forget those fairy tales about the broadly-based curriculum and drive home to your colleagues how to drill your pupils in the art of how to take the test. Forget the frills! All the kiddies have to do is memorise the key facts and some basic language and maths operations, and you'll soon find you're heading for promotion from the Vauxhall Conference.

Bill Clinton used to have a slogan on his campaign office wall which read: 'It's the economy, stupid!' This is reputed to have concentrated most wondrously the minds of his workers on what to get across to the voters, and is still working even more miraculous wonders for Slick Willie. Think what it will do for your results to have on every classroom wall the slogan – 'It's the tests, stupid!' Your job will be to make sure all the galley slaves are toiling suitably under the lash.

Heads are too out of touch to be curricular leaders these days, so volunteer to take responsibility for this area – giving yourself some grandiose title like Deputy Director (Curriculum) – and then think how it will look on your CV to have the biggest league table jump of all time on the record. That should convince some gullible governors somewhere that if you can do it in Grimesville up t'north, you will certainly be able to do it in their more salubrious climes. Because that's where you're intending to head next, as I see from your eminently laudable ambition.

But don't let your undoubtedly short-lived success con you into making the mistake of doing a further spell of missionary work among 'les damnés de la terre'. When it comes to school league tables it well behoves you to remember the immortal words of Damon Runyon: "The race is not always to the swift, nor the battle to the strong – but that's the way to bet."

Politics, deceit and the headteacher

IN RECENT conversations with headteachers, I have been struck by the feeling of so many of them that one of the most fundamental changes in their role in recent years is the way they have been increasingly propelled into the political arena. This is not to deny that heads have always had to be politicians to some extent. If politics is taken to be the art of reaching decisions about contested values, then it is clear that heads, like all other managers, were always politicians by definition.

The changes seem to be that not only are values more contested in the pluralist societies which most developed countries have now become, but crucially that the LEA buffer between heads and the communities outside schools has diminished, if not disappeared, in some respects in recent years. Issues which, in the past, heads could refer to their LEAs (or at least declare to be the concern of the LEA rather than themselves) are reducing in number as local management of schools (LMS) gathers pace, and as 'opting out' and 'site-based management' become more general. Decisions which might, in the past, have been the province of locally elected politicians and their officers in the LEAs are now firmly in the laps of school governors, and *their* chief officer is the headteacher.

In many schools the governors have *de facto* delegated most of these 'political' decisions to the headteachers. This process is likely to be far more difficult for heads than similar developments are for many managers outside education. Heads face a particular dilemma because the lessons of schools and the lessons of politics can diverge considerably in a number of significant ways. To take one of the more obvious points as an example, one of the main purposes of education has traditionally been to show pupils how to search after truth. It is not usually expressed in such grandiose terms, but the introduction to scientific methods of investigation, and the inculcation of the ability to sift evidence, are just two examples of ways in which teachers are attempting to develop pupils' critical faculties so that they can learn to make judgements based (as much as possible) upon sense rather than nonsense. Furthermore, there is a general assumption that schools will attempt to create a moral climate in which, for example, honesty is held up as a virtue to pupils and deceit is, at the very least, discouraged.

Commandments

Nick Tate is not the first to look to schools to teach moral commandments, although most teachers have always maintained that morality is caught rather than taught (which, some would argue, puts much greater pressure on teachers to live 'the moral life'). 'Walking the talk' was an ideal concept familiar to teachers long before the management gurus coined the phrase. Many writers have argued that this has a cumulative effect upon the majority of teachers themselves, who, if they are not morally comparatively good to start with, are actually made good – relative to those in many other occupations – by the nature of the work they undertake.

There is, however, a significant amount of writing about politics which argues that deceit, in this latter field, is not only inevitable but actually essential. This was, of course, one of the central theses of Machiavelli's work, and it is symptomatic of the generally unpalatable nature of his message over the centuries that the adjective 'machiavellian' has come to be attached to the more transparently devious and deceitful politicians, with the implicit assumption that there are others who are telling the truth.

In a more recent body of writing, particularly in his book *The Prevalence of Deceit* in 1991, F.G. Bailey has provided a detailed and authoritative elaboration and development of the arguments of Machiavelli and others, and has reached the very well-argued conclusion that objective truth is unattainable in the practice of politics:

'The very nature of political interaction pushes us back from any serious and sustained effort to ask questions and so find the kind of truth that goes into building bridges, controlling erosion, or even growing tomatoes. In that respect, politics brings about diseducation, discouraging thought and providing authorised, pre-processed answers. The scientific kind of enquiry – how means and ends relate to each other – is inappropriate exactly because politics concern contested values, not the means to attaining some accepted value. Politics, in other words, can never be like a natural science. Politicians, who are by definition contestants to make one or another value prevail, cannot avoid moral questions. Even when they take the trouble to find the "facts", it is only so that they can better impose their own definitions of the right and the good.' (Bailey op.cit. p. 128)

Casualty

Following this line of argument, it is probably more apt to say that truth is the first casualty of politics and (following the dictum of Clausewitz) that war, in this respect as in others, is merely the continuation of politics by other means. Bailey goes further and supports the proposition that society requires for its survival the actual practice of deceit in politics. In our own recent history in the UK, there appears to be an increasing readiness on the part of the public in general to recognise that politicians are at best being 'economical with the truth' a good deal of the time. The *Yes, Minister* and *Yes, Prime Minister* sitcoms were based largely on Talleyrand's premise that speech was given to humans so that they could hide their thoughts – a thesis given added academic weight by Professor Aitchison in her 1996 Reith Lectures on 'The Language Web'. The extension of the idea by the sitcom scriptwriters was that the Sir Humphrey Appleby civil servant character was actually more polished in his ability to disguise the truth under a cloak of words than were the politicians themselves.

In the late 1980s I had the personal experience of serving as a local councillor for four years. The political party which I represented at the election had never been successful in my area before, and is certainly never going to be successful again because it has subsequently departed the national scene (if they're not already lost causes when I join them, they soon go that way). In that minority capacity, I became very quickly aware of the different modes of operation in the academic and the political fields. On the one hand, there I was teaching my students to avoid simplistic 'black and white' answers to complex issues in education, while in the council chambers the arguments which raged backwards and forwards between the two major parties were nearly all of the 'we are completely right, you are totally wrong' variety. I would hardly have been surprised if they had started throwing custard pies at each other.

There is more than a slight touch of the 'holier than thou' about the previous paragraph, but I have little doubt that the representatives of my own party, if it had ever been in office, would have had to conduct their business in ways which would have been frowned upon by the world of academe. Politicians are frequently forced to take decisions based on what they are often only too well aware is inaccurate or inadequate information. Academics adopt superior attitudes to such behaviour but they often do so from positions of conspicuous inaction. Their ability frequently to see all sides of a question and avoid reaching any definite conclusions can appear to politicians, and others, as a trained incapacity to do anything positive. Paul Chambers, when chairman of ICI, was quoted as saying: "Life at a university, with its intellectual and inconclusive discussions at a postgraduate level, is on the whole a bad training for the real world. Only men (sic) of strong character surmount this handicap."

Continuum

It is possible to set up extremes of the political and academic which should be seen, in most cases, as the ends of a continuum along which actual positions will be taken up in particular instances, as shown in Figure 1 below.

By themselves these, and other descriptors which could no doubt readily be added, are caricatures of a reality which is far less simplistic. Nevertheless, they serve a useful purpose as 'ideal types' against which to map that much more complex reality.

It is my contention that headteachers are caught on the horns of this particular dilemma. On the one hand, they frequently share the politicians' impatience with the research findings of academics, which they find all too often ambiguous and which appear to them to have only a long term – if that – application to the day by day realities of managing a school. On the other hand, their own academic training makes them distrust the latest immediate panaceas for education which are trotted out so glibly by the politicians.

Even so, I think that in recent years heads have been pushed towards the political end of the continuum by the pressures to which I have referred. They increasingly operate in a political arena where deceit is essential for survival, but they do so in

Figure 1

Political	Academic
Research to reinforce prejudices	Research to test hypotheses or generate theory
Soundbite arguments	Arguments developed at (sometimes inordinate) length
Open denigration of opponents in public debate	Covert denigration of opponents 'with the greatest respect'
Debate as propaganda	Debate as the search for truth
Production of position papers	Production of research papers
Publication in the popular media	Publication in 'learned journals'
Black and white arguments	Arguments in various shades of grey

many cases with an exceedingly bad conscience. The occupational tendency to deception of the seller of half-truths in the educational marketplace is not one with which many of them are at all comfortable. When we look these days for reasons why so many heads take early retirement, and why headships are increasingly difficult to fill, perhaps we should look to the changes in the nature of the job to which I have alluded. It is perhaps hardly surprising that many teachers of high calibre and integrity are not willing to put their names forward for jobs where they may suspect the ability to dissimulate convincingly will be a prerequisite.

The admissions game

BURSAR: I wonder, headmaster, if we might review our admissions policy in the light of the recent investigative survey carried out on your behalf by the school's admissions watchdog committee?

HEADMASTER: Yes, this would seem an opportune moment. Just refresh my memory with the main findings, will you old chap?

B: Well, there are the 82 families we have identified who claimed to live in what used to be loosely described as our catchment area, but who we discovered gave false addresses at the time they made applications to send their offspring to the school.

H: Oh, yes. Some of them were quite ingenious in this respect, weren't they?

B: Indeed, headmaster. Some of them made, what I understand are called on the stock exchange, multiple applications. They claimed to live at up to four different addresses to cover any eventuality if we drew up a geographical zoning policy.

H: But they were the relatively easy ones to spot from the first sieving of the applications, weren't they? There were much more devious sharp practices than that.

B: Quite. I suppose the crop of marital breakdowns might come into the 'slightly more cunning' category. You will recall the pattern: traumatic separation; one parent, accompanied by child, moves into a flat in the immediate vicinity of the school; then a sudden reconciliation and it's back to the family home immediately after the successful application for the son or daughter to enter the school.

H: Yes, I thought that was a class above just 'borrowing' friends' addresses for the application period. That was an easy one to spot. The staff detective agency conclusively proved that no child ever entered or departed from some of the houses concerned. Mind you, I'm not happy about Mr. Jenkins moonlighting by doing surveillance for the Social Security on the side. I understand, though, that some of our local residents are doing a similarly lucrative trade in 'selling' their addresses for the duration. One has to admit that some of the fake 'exchange of contracts' documents were beautifully produced. Next year we might try setting a few more difficult hurdles for them to jump by asking for proof of long-term rental going back at least a year. They're already aware that we're cross-checking addresses against the electoral roll, I take it?

B: Oh yes, they're already cooking up dodges to get round that. False council tax booklets are already changing hands for serious money. I understand they're pricier than forged passports on the local black market.

H: I have to admit that what really intrigues me is the shameless lengths to which some people are apparently prepared to go to use the religious foundation of the school as a back-door means of entry.

B: Yes, I gather some of the parish priests in the region have expressed some anxieties about the true sincerity of the increasing number of mid-life conversions to our faith. I think many of our parents these days have a great deal in common with the late, lamented Groucho Marx, who said how important sincerity was as a personal attribute in the modern world, and how you had it made if you could fake it.

(Much sardonic laughter on both sides.)

H: Regular church attendance is certainly insufficient evidence of piety these days.

B: No – even the baptism and confirmation criteria aren't enough, because they're all into those rituals now. When this lot have got their eye on the main chance, they'll take anything in their stride.

H: But you have to admit that promising to send the fruit of your loins on a daily pilgrimage of 20 miles each way, with self-flagellation as an optional extra, is quite a commitment.

B: Well, it's certainly an advance on simply shipping them in from the next county by personally chauffeured taxi service.

H: Then there's the entrance examination itself.

B: You mean the growing number of cases where 'ghost writers' have been identified?

H: Yes. That's a ruse which is a real danger to our league table position if those who pass aren't the same as those who turn up in September. Do you think the tattooing procedures will nip that dodge in the bud?

B: Good question. Personally I thought the fingerprint checks would do the trick, but they were very quickly wise to that one. I think we're going to have to go the whole way with DNA testing if we're to have a chance of outsmarting them in this area. Thank heavens they're not into cloning as yet.

H: It was so much simpler and straightforward in the good old days, don't you think?

B: You mean when the parents just turned up for an interview with bundles of used fivers in brown envelopes?

H: Of course. It didn't matter about league tables and things like that back then. That's why it's so important to interview the children themselves these days, and why we have to eliminate the 'ringer' problem. What with that, and the dope testing we had to introduce, we've learned a lot from our friends in the horse racing fraternity.

B: True, but it gets harder and harder to spot the ones who've been to the interview training crammers. The lie detector machines proved useless years ago against their cunning subterfuges.

H: Yes, but at least you can very quickly tell from the interviews if there's any danger of lowering the tone of the school by getting a few 'wrong uns' who have slipped through the net.

B: So all in all, then, you're not totally dissatisfied with our attempts to raise the fences against our scheming and duplicitous parental clientele?

H: No, quite the contrary. As long as we make it just that bit more difficult each year for them to cheat and swindle their offspring into the school, I think we can rest assured that only the most guileful, affluent and unprincipled of the middle class will have any chance at all of seeing their children enter our sacred portals. That should keep out the horny-handed lower orders, who haven't much of an idea of the rules of our game, never mind how to bend them. We must keep them firmly in their place, as clients of their local sink schools, in what I like to think of as 'the valley of the clueless'. Heaven forbid that we should ever have to accept the sons and daughters of the naïve and penurious working classes.

B: Quite, headmaster.

The head as spin doctor

Y OU CAN tell I've been in this game a long time because I can remember the days when the majority of headteachers wanted to have nothing at all to do with the media. However, in these days of market forces, competitive edges and schools as brand leaders, heads know that favourable publicity in the media is worth its weight in extra pupil numbers and the resources that go with them. PR doesn't just mean (good) public relations these days – it means press releases and all the proactive efforts of that kind in order to put your school on the (right) map. The problem remains, though, that the original reason why heads wanted to steer clear of the once dreaded newshounds still stands. As far as the media are concerned, bad news is good news.

Back in my own days as a pupil at school, I recall two incidents which helped to shape my own long term view of the media. The first concerned a train crash at Harrow and Wealdstone railway station in 1952 in which 122 passengers died when the Perth-Euston sleeping car express went through three signals at 'danger' and ploughed into the back of a local commuter train. This remains the second worst accident in British railway history. Shortly afterwards an English teacher came in to teach us one morning, visibly shaken by the story he had been told by one of his friends who worked for a national newspaper. It transpired that, on the evening when the news of the train disaster came through to the press room, it had so far been what was then referred to as a 'slow news' night. When the editor received the news, his very audible and very jubilant instant reaction had been to say: "Thank God!" The fact that this was then regarded by some colleagues as going a teeny weeny bit over the top shows how far has been the journey of media cynicism which has taken us to *Drop The Dead Donkey's* presentation of life behind the scenes in the newsroom.

The second incident was when I had occasion to be at a careers convention at Belle Vue Zoo, as it then was, in Manchester, the morning after what had been blazoned across the press as a large fire in the big cats' house. I remember having my withers well and truly wrung by newspaper stories of how zookeepers had wept as they had to put down their animal charges as humanely as possible before the fire condemned the animals to a worse death. So I duly trotted along, in best schoolboy rubbernecking mode, to see the results of the conflagration, only to find very little damage indeed. Further enquiries revealed that there had been a fair bit of smoke, not much fire, and one old tiger had expired from what appeared to be heart failure during the rumpus.

Natural causes

Later, during my own teaching career, I had a biology teacher colleague who once unwisely accepted the 'gift' of a caretaker's cat which had died in old age of natural causes. He used this dead animal in a demonstration of dissection with some of the upper school pupils. How the story got to the press we never discovered, but its presentation in one Sunday newspaper was of pupils being *forced* to cut open their old pet, which had been killed for the purpose, and of their weeping buckets in the process. This was a single sex secondary school in a part of town, where any suggestion of shedding a tear among the very likely lads in question would have immediately put them into 'big girl's blouse' territory. Furthermore, my colleague was probably the most popular teacher in the school at the time and the lads themselves were really incensed at the spin the newspaper had put on the story.

I well remember one of the boys concerned angrily assuring me that they had never even noticed the cat during its lifetime, let alone considered it to be a 'pet'. Nevertheless, this particular teacher became the recipient of some very nasty hate mail for quite a time after the general public had read of him as some potential vivisectionist.

So newspapers thrived then, as now, not only on bad news but often on invented (or at the very least highly distorted) bad news. As someone somewhere once put it: 'Newspaper reporters don't sell the truth; they sell newspapers.'' So if you, as a head, are approached for an interview on some aspect of your school's record which could just conceivably be portrayed in a bad light, what are you going to do about it?

No comment . . .

Your first reaction may be to declare that you are unavailable for comment. This is not a wise move on two counts. Firstly you will probably find this has become part of the headline for the story: **'STENCHVILLE SECONDARY SCHOOL SCANDAL: HEADTEACHER UNAVAILABLE FOR COMMENT.'** This does not look at all good to the local citizenry, who may well conclude that you are personally entirely responsible for the 'scandal'.

If you are really unlucky, the story will be accompanied by an old photo from the files which shows you entering the school with your face partially obscured behind a newspaper. This could have a witty caption alongside such as **'ENTER THE TEFLON HEAD: NO CHARGE EVER STICKS**!' By this stage, the good ratepayers of the parish will have concluded that, although the original story was about your exclusion of some pupil on the grounds that he or she was into biting classmates' ears, Mike Tyson style, the *real* story is that you have been hiring out the gym and the fourth year girls for the making of porno movies.

The second reason why being unavailable for comment is not the smartest of moves is that you can bet your life that there will be many others only too willing to be available for comment. Putting your self at the mercy of others' comments is unwise, to say the least. Do you *really* want your chair of governors to speak on behalf of the school? Even statements of so-called support can be double edged. 'We are firmly behind the head' is ambiguous enough as it stands, but if it is followed by 'We have always believed in giving full autonomy to the head, who must be allowed total accountability for her actions' then you're really for the high jump if things start to go seriously pear-shaped.

But what the chair of governors may say will be as nothing compared to what reporters can coax out of pupils. For a few used fivers they will supply an instant riot at the most convenient location for the zoom lenses of the local paparazzi. They will also throw in a few lines for good measure about your nickname being 'Dracula' or whatever the reporter thinks will best suit the alliteration in the headline.

This will be unlikely to boost your falling rolls and, if it did, would you really want the kind of pupil who is attracted by the prospect of blood-sucking on the curriculum? Moreover, it may well result in rapid follow-up visits from Ofsted, whose chief does not have a reputation for being either camera or publicity shy. Ministers of Education may also rush to demand explanations so they can appear on Newsnight (on Jeremy Paxman's side for once).

Media management

So you've got to speak to the reporters, if only to keep them away from their other potential prey. Now the trick is the degree to which you can control the interview, and even more so what is written up afterwards. This is known as media management. But your opportunities for spin doctoring may at first sight appear somewhat limited. You may think that having a large tape recorder (preferably of the old obsolete reel-to-reel kind) conspicuously playing on your desk while you are being interviewed might just give you something of an edge when it comes to what is written up afterwards, but it is not likely to put you on a good footing with the reporter. He or she may pay you back for this by noting when the tape stops running and then asking you some apparently irrelevant question about what you think about the local councillors.

If you're fairly non-committal, you may find yourself being asked a more leading question which implies that it's well known they're all taking bribes. If you then fall into the trap of saying that just because there have been some well documented cases of councillors on the take, you don't for one moment think that any of the local variety are actually crooked, you will probably wake up to a headline which states: **'LOCAL HEAD SAYS IT IS WELL DOCUMENTED THAT COUNCILLORS ARE ON THE TAKE!'**

It's no good your complaining about this to the reporter, or threatening to take him or her before the Press Council (a really dire threat which should have the said reporter rolling in the aisles!), because the response will always be that it's some anonymous sub-editor who writes the headlines. (Who do you think writes the titles for these columns of mine? I should be so lucky!)

Perhaps the best illustration of the apparently innocuous remark to the press becoming the headline from hell concerns an Anglican bishop paying his first visit to the USA in the 1930s. Arriving by liner as was then the custom, he was met at the end of the gangplank by a New York newshound who had obviously been primed to ask him a question about a big scandal story of the time. "What do you think of the brothels on the East Side, bishop?" was the question. The bishop had obviously seen this one coming and thought he had neatly sidestepped the question by responding: "*Are* there any brothels on the East Side?" The headline in the newspaper in question the following morning was: **'BISHOP'S FIRST QUESTION ON ARRIVING IN NEW YORK: ARE THERE ANY BROTHELS ON THE EAST SIDE?'**

Keeping it under control

If even the words you *do* utter can be taken down and used in false evidence against you, maybe the tape recorder ploy isn't such a good idea after all. So what can you do to keep some feeling of well-being both during and after the interview? You can speak slowly for starters. If you can adjust to the pace at which the reporter can take it all down, you give less scope for the misquotations which can strangely enough become the main thrust of the published news item.

Secondly, you should not take the bait and the hook of supplying gratuitous comment of the kind that landed people in trouble with the headlines in the previous paragraph. Reporters don't talk about going on 'fishing trips' for no reason. If complimented on your car in the head's parking space outside, don't volunteer the fact that it's a German-made 1.8 GTI turbo charged 12 series with double overhead cam and cabriolet top, etc. The reporter may be driving a Lada (although it's unlikely), and envy may spark off a story that begins: 'At a time when Stenchville Secondary's finances are at an all time low, it seems somewhat surprising that the Michael Schumacher of the local heads has yet again upgraded his Formula One racer.'

Thirdly, limit the time you are available for interview and make sure the reporter is escorted from the premises immediately afterwards by your secretary – unless you can't trust your secretary (but if you can't trust your secretary, any precautions are a complete waste of time because you're already dead in the water).

Politician tricks

If the reporter should start the interview not with 'fishing trip' try-ons but with all guns blazing and a question such as: "Why are your school's finances the subject of a council enquiry?" you've just got to fall back on the expertise you have acquired by listening on your car radio every morning to politicians handling such questions on the *Today* programme. What do they do when confronted by really tough questions like this? That's it! They simply answer a question that wasn't asked in the first place but which they think will put them in a better light. In other words, waffle on as high a moral plain as you can reach, implying all the while that anyone who could possibly dream of asking such a question must emanate from some low-life planet of which you're glad to say you've never even heard.

A distraction device may be handy here. Have a story already prepared which involves some of your pupils (who just happen to be bringing the reporter a cup of tea and biscuits at that very moment). You will commend them in the reporter's presence on having rescued some sick puppies from unimaginable squalor and degradation and you will imply that they thoroughly deserve to receive suitable publicity – if not a medal – for the said rescue. With any luck, the reporter will quickly realise this will sell infinitely more papers than the state of your school's finances and he or she may be instantly and totally distracted, particularly if the pupils are suitably photogenic (and if they aren't, then the puppies certainly will be). This is known as giving the reporter other fish to fry, and perhaps your skills as a spin doctor aren't all that limited after all. Sometimes, just sometimes, good bad news is better than bad bad news.

The mailed fist in the not so velvet glove

WILLARD WALLER, in his classic book *Sociology of Teaching*, wrote some 65 years ago that schools were based on the authority principle and that this authority was constantly threatened. In Waller's view, schools were established according to an autocratic, hierarchical pattern and heads were obliged to act in authoritarian ways; but the authority of the head was threatened because there were other groups who wanted to achieve their own ends in education. These groups inevitably found that at some times, and on some issues, the head would oppose their particular interests, and the resentment they felt at being thwarted led them to try to undermine the head's authority in the hope of still getting their own way. Among the groups which Waller listed were parents, pupils, staff and governing bodies (although he used the American terms current at the time rather than their English counterparts).

Schools in the USA have a long history of vulnerability to the pressures of internal and external communities, and the School Board was something to be, if not feared, then at least approached with extreme caution by principals. Waller made his analysis at a time when English heads may have felt considerably less threatened than their American counterparts; in those days, governing bodies in the UK were little more than rubber stamps for headteacher actions. I suspect, however, that this comparison would no longer seem as favourable to most English heads. The pressures towards public accountability, combined with at least the lip service paid to democratic trends since World War Two, have made some of the Victorian heads in the UK seem like characters from a bygone age of very long ago.

Dictatorial

Historians of education have well chronicled the way in which many late nineteenth-century heads apparently wielded what amounted to dictatorial powers in a quite open and arbitrary fashion. Thring, the then head of Uppingham School, could notoriously declare: "I am supreme here and will permit no interference". What was then, to him at least, merely a statement of fact, would nowadays seem like an idle boast if any headteacher were foolish enough to make it. However, Thring and his contemporaries ruled their public and endowed schools in the same despotic ways that many employers of the age ruled their factories and workshops. Pupils could be flogged, and teachers sacked, at the whim of the autocrat in charge, who was fully expected to rule with a rod of iron. The historian of Oundle School wrote of its nineteenth century headmaster, Sanderson, that staff "must see eye to eye with him; if they did not they must go."

Behaviour and attitudes of such a kind nowadays, if they became publicly known, would land a headteacher out of a job and at least into the local rag, if not the local clink, in no time at all. Yet heads are still expected by society to act on its behalf to ensure that those measures currently favoured by the majority in power are speedily implemented (and sometimes the speed of that implementation is expected to be breakneck, with little concern for whose neck gets broken in the process). That majority can, of course, dramatically shift from the right to the left of the political spectrum (or vice versa) and, in the process of such political shifts, certain interest groups will find their own positions reinforced or weakened. Either way, they may redouble their efforts to influence the actions of the head in their favour.

So what can the average headteacher do to exercise the power and authority officially vested in the position in order to get things done without giving anyone, either inside or outside of the school, the excuse of tyrannical misrule as grounds for dismissal?

The answer from most teachers would be 'quite a lot', if recent research conducted in the USA[1] by Angela Spaulding is to be believed. Teaching staff in 26 cities in five states were asked: 'what do teachers need to know in order to understand and survive life in the classroom?' Their answers were overwhelmingly directed neither to curricular knowledge nor teaching skills; their main concern was to know how to identify and respond to the political manoeuvrings or strategies of the school principal. This appears to have been something of a shock to Ms Spaulding. As it has, however, been a leitmotif in my own writing for many a long year, I am not at all surprised to have yet more research confirmation of my own empirical findings in these respects (this is the accepted academic format for what lesser mortals might term prejudice reinforcement or the 'I told you so' syndrome).

What follows could be read as a guide for the headteacher, based on this research, on how to nurture the autocracy plant so that it continues to flourish under the somewhat more difficult growing conditions of modern times. It could also be read as a guide on how to treat teachers with very thinly veiled contempt, with detrimental consequences for the quality of the teaching and learning in the school.

Pretence

Pretending to consult on decisions already taken is one well-known way of hiding the mailed fist in the velvet glove, but it is fascinating to read of some of the current American variants of this practice. One teacher recounts how his principal runs the school with the aid of his chief barons, who are the heads of the five biggest departments in the school. The principal holds private and unannounced meetings of 'the Big 5' at which the decisions are taken on which the rest of the staff are going to be subsequently

'consulted'. This even extends to the heads of the other departments. To quote our source:

"Then he calls for a departmental chairperson meeting (there are five other departments besides the Big 5) and presents issues as if they are being presented for the first time. Solutions and policies are presented by everyone at the meeting, but the only solutions and policies that are ever carried out are those that the Big 5 have previously decided. How do I know these things? I *am* one of the Big 5."

This syndrome is not by any means restricted to American schools. Anyone familiar with the workings of local government in the UK will instantly recognise that phenomenon known as the 'caucus meeting' at which the issues later to be debated in all apparent openness and transparency in the council chambers are well and truly 'stitched up' in advance by the ruling group. Thus is democracy habitually subverted.

Shenanigans ·

The resemblance to party political shenanigans is indicative of the ways in which modern heads use political strategies to achieve the same ends that their Victorian predecessors might have reached by more direct and brutal means. The latter despots probably

89

didn't need to surround themselves with barons. It's only weaker tyrants who look to lesser warlords for support, although inner circles have always had their attraction for the otherwise lonely dictator. Even Stalin had an inner circle – except that in his case it was constantly changing, and when you left his inner circle there was no outer circle except the Lubyanka prison and execution. It appears he had the disconcertingly paranoid habit of leading up to yet another purge by saying to his apparent acolytes, quite out of the blue, such things as: "You are not looking Comrade Stalin straight in the eye today. Why do you avert your gaze?" This must have been a more alarming way of discovering you were for the chop than anything I have ever encountered with headteachers.

Returning to our American teachers, they allege that another strategy of principals for getting their own way is to favour the yes-men and women and bring down retribution on the heads of anyone who dares to oppose their will:

"Teachers feel that some principals 'definitely have favourites' and that these people get special treatment. Teachers state that those who receive favoured status in their schools go on trips, teach fewer classes than others, and get a bigger share of capital outlay than the others, and the list goes on."

Contrast this with what Angela Spaulding terms principals who 'flex their muscles'. These are principals who use what teachers consider to be improper means of getting their own way:

"If someone disagrees with our principal, they are quickly reminded that they can ask for a transfer. Of course, this kind of suggestion is put in a joking way but we all know it is not a joke."

Sometimes retribution comes in more tangible forms, such as one principal insisting on seeing detailed lesson plans, from those who have challenged his rulings, which he makes clear will be checked by him personally. This approach is best summed up by another teacher in the following way:

"If we don't back off, our principal shows us just how tough our jobs could become."

Bullying

It is hardly surprising that teachers who claim to have spoken up against their principal report that after such retribution they are now much less vocal and more apprehensive about a confrontation. A further level of concern about all this is that the teachers feel that what clearly amounts to bullying of this sort often has detrimental effects not only on the teachers themselves but on the quality of their teaching and the pupils' consequent learning. Teachers under this kind of regime report that they are made to feel nervous, incompetent, distrusted and under constant observation. They describe heads who are always checking on teachers' performance in the classroom as 'micro-managing'. As one teacher reports:

"I think our principal does it just to be mean. He seems to enjoy making others sweat. It is bewildering to think he has so much time to micro-manage us."

There is much, much more of this kind of reaction in Angela Spaulding's research and I may well draw upon it in later articles in *Managing Schools Today*. It does appear to confirm that while heads in general may *appear* far less despotic than their predecessors in times gone by, the autocratic design of school authority has not disappeared but has merely been cloaked by the language of democracy. Teachers in the USA have apparently learned not to listen to this language itself but to the messages behind it:

"When we have faculty meetings and the principal is speaking you can tell by his voice inflection, body language etc., what he wants. Even if he doesn't say so or even if his verbal message contradicts his non-verbal. We have learned to read his body language."

Or as another two teachers in different schools put it:

"Our principal does this. He says one thing but means another. We all know it. It is a game we play along with. He does it to get what he wants."

"We hear what she says and then hear what she means, because if our principal does not get her way you know life will be tough

91

for a while. We go along with it usually because it is worse if we refuse or challenge her."

Astute

This means that some heads still have plenty of opportunities to (mis)use their considerable powers to silence or cow their subordinates, although they have to go about their autocratic business these days in ways which are more politically astute. The headteacher from hell now needs to be familiar with the full range of machiavellian strategies. Overt brutality is currently out of fashion, but Willard Waller's analysis still apparently holds good for many an oppressive principal in the USA.

Anonymous contributions from teachers to the educational press would lead us to believe that this is also the case with bullying headteachers here in the UK. If so, then to what extent are heads forced to resort to such tactics by the pressures upon them? The American study concluded that such leadership behaviour was ineffective, and there is a lot more evidence to suggest that schools where teachers in general feel oppressed are not good examples of 'learning organisations'. We nevertheless need to find out if it is the system itself which makes some heads feel that they have to behave in these ways. There are also uncomfortable questions to be answered, such as whether it is in the interests of the pupils and their learning that *some* teachers have to be bullied by their heads?

Reference
1. Angela Spaulding, writing in the journal *School Leadership and Management*, Vol. 17 No. 1 1997 pp. 39-55 (I am happy to acknowledge that this chapter draws very considerably on her research).

Pressure down the line

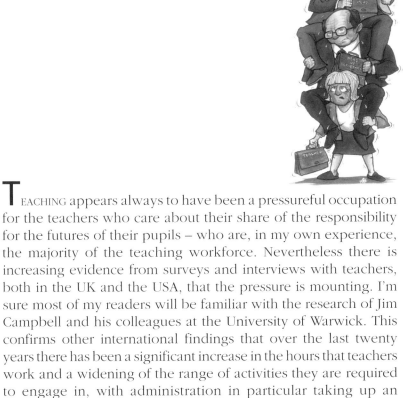

Teaching appears always to have been a pressureful occupation for the teachers who care about their share of the responsibility for the futures of their pupils – who are, in my own experience, the majority of the teaching workforce. Nevertheless there is increasing evidence from surveys and interviews with teachers, both in the UK and the USA, that the pressure is mounting. I'm sure most of my readers will be familiar with the research of Jim Campbell and his colleagues at the University of Warwick. This confirms other international findings that over the last twenty years there has been a significant increase in the hours that teachers work and a widening of the range of activities they are required to engage in, with administration in particular taking up an increasing amount of their time.

To some extent this only reflects a general trend towards what has been termed the *intensification* of work across a whole range of 'middle class' occupations. A survey of white-collar workers published in *Management Today* in the Summer of 1998 produced much evidence of a widespread feeling of being overworked, with managements demanding more and more 'overtime' either in the office or at home. Indeed, family life at home appeared increasingly to be badly affected to the point of highly stressed interpersonal relations and broken marriages.

The number of articles in the press which picked up on this survey, and the letters which ensued, suggested that this research had touched on a very raw nerve indeed in current society. So what I am going to concentrate upon in this chapter – the way that pressures towards work intensification, and demands for tangible results which can be measured and presented in performance tables, are passed down the chain of command – is not unique to teaching.

The better researched crime novels are very good at describing how police forces are pressured all the way 'down the line' to achieve 'quotas' instigated at the top of the line by the politicians of the day (see John Harvey's 'Resnick' novels for good examples). But perhaps teachers, by comparison, have a particular problem in passing the pressures they experience further down the line. There is a difference between police officers being constantly exhorted to get tough on criminals (as well as crime and the causes of crime, to coin a phrase) and teachers who are genuinely concerned about the children they teach. These teachers may well feel it is unethical to pass the pressures they experience on to the children in their care.

Teachers' voices

The point is illustrated by teachers' voices quoted in the UK by Sharon Gewirz[1] and in the USA by Angela Spaulding[2]. Gewirz is very good at analysing, through her interview data, the precise ways in which teachers are driven to use every possible time slot during the school day to increase the examination and test results of their pupils. It is not difficult to imagine the tones of the voices of the UK teachers behind the following quotations:

- "There are days when I leave here and I haven't stood still for a second and I haven't had one minute to myself to even go to the toilet or to just think."
- "If you go to our staffroom at lunchtime you won't find anybody in it at all . . . Jesus, years ago, that was the main collective point.

Now what happens is that everybody . . . stays in their own (department) working."

It will be no consolation (though perhaps a surprise) to the many teachers whose school staffrooms have ceased to be the temporary decompression chambers of yesteryear, that I can report exactly the same phenomenon in the staffroom of my own faculty in higher education. This often now reminds me, at what are supposed to be the breaks during the day, of that mysteriously deserted yacht, the *Marie Celeste*. A few used polystyrene coffee holders from a snatched (breakfast?) drink on arrival in the early morning are often the only testimony that living human beings once passed this way. The university SCRs of most current TV drama are, I'm afraid, as anachronistic as the mortar boards and gowns of the teachers in children's comics. Perhaps that's what the Nottingham police also feel about the Resnick novels, but somehow I don't think so.

Gewirz analyses in sharp focus the demands the new systems of control in education have imposed upon teachers. She depicts the teachers' resentment at the extent to which recording and monitoring pupils' work in the formal ways now required take them away from what they see as the real work of teaching – preparing lessons, interacting with students both within and outside the classroom, and marking. She shows how teachers feel pressured to target particular groups of pupils in secondary schools (e.g. those at the threshhold of attaining C grades at GCSE).

This targeting involves not only providing revision sessions during breaks, but also adopting excessively didactic pedagogical practices during normal class time, even when other approaches might be more important for the long term education of the class as a whole, or even for immediate class interest and consequent behaviour.

As far as the management of all this is concerned, Gewirz writes as follows:

'Like the other headteachers in our study, one of Mrs Carnegie's responses to league tables, inspection and the generally competitive climate within which most schools are now operating is to install hierarchically structured systems of accountability.

At Martineau School, classroom teachers are accountable to "heads of cluster", who in turn are accountable to the "senior teacher link" and the headteacher. These clear lines of accountability, coupled with appraisal systems, effectively regulate the work of teachers, ensuring that the values of the performance-driven market are institutionalised to the extent that they penetrate classroom practice.'

Please note that this is accountability in one direction only – upwards.

American views

The voices of the teachers in the USA whom Spaulding quotes show that teachers often have the feeling that, although their support is demanded as a right by their superiors, there is not a corresponding sense of support for them by these same superiors. This, I suspect, is one of the keys to the feelings of exhaustion and early burn-out experienced by too many teachers currently. I quote the American research because there is nothing recent that I am aware of in the UK material which is quite as vivid. However, I think the sentiments expressed apply equally well in both cultures; indeed, they may well be universal in those situations where workers feel unsupported by management. The view that loyalty ought to be a two-way process is not confined to the USA.

One of the teachers talks about discipline problems, as so many teachers everywhere understandably do:

"This can then cause an explosive situation between the student and the teacher if the administration has not taken time to intervene or just informs the teacher that there is no time for the problem or doesn't care and they must handle their own problems. If the principal gives the teacher certain responsibilities this becomes very stressful as the decision will become the teacher's decision alone."

Out of Spaulding's sample of 62 teachers, 54 said they did not feel that their principal was supportive of them personally or professionally. The following quotations sum up their feelings:

- "Tell me where is the principal who will say,'I will stand behind you – right or wrong – in front of the public'. You can't find one."
- "Our principal does not back teachers, she is not interested in what happens in our classrooms."
- "You better hope you never have a crisis situation in our building, you would never find the principal."
- "Support? What support? It is simply not there."

The effect that this can have on teachers is shown by the following statement:

"I get so beat down with all the negatives of teaching. Students and parents seem to always be fighting educators about one thing or another. Everyone seems to think they are an exception. And if I take a hard line, I am the one who loses – I end up with egg on my face because the principal won't back my stand. So I don't feel I stand for anything any more. Personally I don't feel worth much, professionally I know I am not accomplishing much."

Market forces

My own view is that many of these school principals are in the same self-preservation society as the majority of the working population. In Western democracies there has been a trend towards politicians demanding more of the workforce by also demanding more of those who manage them. This has intensified since the collapse of Communism in the former USSR. Before that, those who managed societies based on market forces had to temper those forces lest people look to the alternative model. Now there's no longer any alternative, they can let the market forces rip. Heads in the UK have therefore been put under intense pressures to show that their schools are climbing the league tables. Nowhere has this been more clearly expressed than by Anthea Millett, chief executive of the TTA, in her speech to the annual BEMAS conference:

"Soft-hearted heads who were too close to their staff will be toughened up with new leadership courses. They would be taught how to drive their staff harder to meet their personal and school targets and get better results."[3]

So heads are told by those holding high office to pressure their staff to 'perform'. In the worst cases it's all pressure and no support. Pupils' results may show short term gains, but there are going to be long-term prices to pay as we kill off the geese that lay the golden eggs.

The reader may feel I have over-concentrated on the secondary sector here, but the same pressures are now being inexorably exerted on the primary sector. Even John Harvey's pressured policeman can see the effects of all this on teachers when he spends a day investigating in the inner city primary schools in the 1992 novel *Off Minor*. The intensification of the teacher's working day is quickly brought home to him:

'By three-thirty Naylor was exhausted and thought he now knew why so many teachers had the appearance of marathon runners. Losers, at that.' (p.124)

Do we really want exhausted and losing marathon runners working with our children? Where are their supportive trainers?

References

1. Sharon Gewirz (1997), 'Post-welfarism and the reconstruction of teachers' work in the UK' in *Education Policy* Vol. 12 No. 4, pp 217-231.
2. Angela Spaulding (1997), 'Life in Schools – a qualitative study of teacher perspectives on the politics of principals: ineffective leadership behaviors and their consequences upon teacher thinking and behavior' in *School Leadership and Management* Vol. 17 No.1 pp. 39-55.
3. Anthea Millett quoted in *Education Journal*, October 1997.

Whispering in the head's ear

THE SCHOOL deputy head has been a figure much more in the forefront of writing on education management in recent years. Geoff Southworth has argued convincingly in numerous publications for a redefinition of the deputy role in primary schools. He prefers the term 'assistant head' for the kind of pro-active co-managing figure he has in mind. What he is deploring is the fact that many a deputy head in the primary school is just that – someone who occasionally deputises for the absent head, but otherwise has very little to do with the leadership and direction of the school. In one of Southworth's recent surveys, many primary deputies felt that they were allocated insufficient non-contact time to play a co-leadership role effectively, even when the head expected them to perform in that way. They were constantly torn between their teaching and managerial duties.

Other writers would prefer the term 'associate head' to be used for similar reasons, and Neville West has written about the ideal headteacher/deputy relationship as a partnership where they are 'co-pilots' of the school. The reality, as evidenced by most research surveys, shows the deputy as an air hostess attending to routine administrative chores on board with drinks trolley and

sick bags to the ready. If the head is absent from the cockpit, the plane simply goes onto automatic pilot as the deputy hasn't much of a clue in which direction they're supposed to be heading. (This rather assumes that the head does!)

Scrutiny

At the same time, the deputy role in secondary schools in particular has been coming under greater scrutiny as economies are sought on the staffing budget. The non-replacement of one or more deputies for this reason has become commonplace in recent years. In the primary sector, there has been a discernible trend to postpone the re-appointment to what is usually the single deputy post once it has been vacated. This development has grown to such an extent that some commentators are now beginning to argue a case for removing that tier of management altogether.

To some degree this is only a belated response to the widespread trend towards 'delayering' in industry and commerce. Organisations in those sectors have stripped out whole tiers of middle management in the search for 'flatter' management structures. And despite the protestations from the management gurus about the miraculous advances in morale, etc. from flattening hierarchies, I strongly suspect that the underlying motives were often the same in the private sector as they are now in the public sector. Cost reduction is probably more often than not the real name of the game wherever delayering occurs.

In this chapter and the next, I would like to make an unfashionable case in favour of the deputy role at all levels of schooling and beyond, on the grounds that if deputies are doing their job properly then they provide an invaluable managerial service to the head and the school. (For purposes of brevity and clarity I am henceforth going to refer to 'the deputy' in the singular in relation to any one school, while accepting that the reality, particularly in the secondary sector, is often more plural and more complex.)

Good tidings . . . and bad

First, and perhaps foremost, the deputy should be able to convey both bad news and good news to the head with equal skill. It requires infinitely more subtlety to perform either service well than most people imagine. To take the good news first, it may seem as if there is no problem at all in spreading glad tidings of comfort and joy, but this is not the case. If the deputy bears too many tales of good cheer to the head then the latter, if possessed of any managerial wisdom, may soon begin to wonder if this messenger doth protest too much. An overdose of good news can be as dangerous for the head as a surfeit of lampreys was for a king with digestive problems. For one thing, this provision of a superfluity of goodies can easily become a form of sycophancy.

The deputy is not there to be a fawning flunky, telling the head only what he or she wants to hear. It is perfectly possible to be a loyal deputy without becoming obsequious. I have written elsewhere (see *The Headteacher from Hell and Other Animals*) on the temptations of using flattery as a means of getting into the head's good books, and the deputy who insists on continuing to write only complimentary notices in those books is doing the head a grave disservice. There is a real warning here to heads who rely solely on deputies for news. The wise head has wider sources of information, among which personal direct observation should be paramount.

Praise where it's due

This is not to say that to avoid this potential pitfall the deputy should never praise the head for a job well done. Heads can be lonely figures who, in many cases, need to have their self-esteem boosted from time to time if and when such boosting is thoroughly justified. It is very difficult for members of staff lower down the pecking order to do this without appearing to be 'crawling' or 'creeping' or whatever the current vogue term. The deputy who has acquired a deserved reputation for 'telling it like it is', on the other hand, is in a position from which it is possible to give praise when praise is due. The deputy who ducks this task through fear of appearing to toady is just as remiss as the one who runs away from the Cassandra-like role of prophet of doom which I will go on to describe.

Indeed, this giving of deserved approbation is not just a possibility but an obligation of the deputy's office. I repeat, however, that this can only be done well by someone who is prepared to carry the bad as well as the good news from Ghent to Aix. The trickiest bad news of all is that which conveys the message that the head could be handling things differently for the benefit of all concerned. Few heads welcome such information, but some are more unwelcoming than others!

There are, unfortunately, a lot of messengers who are so anxious not to be shot that they avoid as much as possible the role of the bearer of bad news (heads who have deputies like this should, however, begin to ask themselves why – maybe shooting deputies regularly from the hip isn't such a good idea after all). This is usually not too calamitous if it relates to cock-ups which have already occurred, because they are bound to come to the attention of the head eventually by some route or other. A worse scenario, however, is when the deputy either leads, or aids and abets, a cover-up of the aforesaid events. This only means that the problem will take even longer to come to the head's attention, by which time it may be too late even to attempt some damage limitation. But the real disaster is when the deputy fails to warn of *impending* calamities which they are in a position to spot long before these approaching whirlwinds can become visible to the head. The deputy is much closer in most schools to the 'grass roots' opinions amongst the staff and has a duty to report to the head when discontent is reaching unusual proportions. If this is tantamount to acting as the 'boss's nark', then so be it. I would prefer to refer to this as the essential intermediary role of the deputy.

Conduit

Most staff realise anyway that any deputy worthy of the name has a duty to act as a conduit to the head, and the shrewd teacher will act accordingly whether the underlying motives for action are good or bad. Indeed, such teachers may also think that deputies who do not make heads aware that the natives are restless are failing in their duties. It is, of course, also the deputy's job to sort out the petty whinges from the real grievances when it comes to reporting back on what the rumour mill is grinding out this week. The natives may wish to convey the impression of restlessness at all times if they think this is a way of wringing a continuous series of concessions out of management. 'Staff morale is at an all-time low' is a message that deputies hear on all too many occasions.

One message you can bet your sweet life will never be transmitted by the staff is that morale is at an all-time high. The allegation of low morale is an electric fence against 'management', meant to stop them encroaching further into what is seen as staff territory. The beauty of the low morale deterrent is that nobody can accurately measure it. It may just mean: 'I personally am far from gruntled just at present and I will take this out on you by alleging that staff morale in general reflects my current mood.'

Once in a while, however, it might just be true that the general situation on the other side of the electric fence may really be going critical. Spotting that occasion when it would be useful to report back to the head before the mutiny actually takes off is the real art of deputyship. Fletcher Christian has not gone down in history as a good deputy on board the Bounty, even if the odd historian thinks the mutineers had a case. (Maybe Captain Bligh needed some different forms of management training?)

Back seat whispers

Equally, it may be that when the head is 'on a roll', as they say these days, and one success follows on another, the deputy may feel obliged to play the other kind of role, as formerly played by Roman slaves. This was the bit part at Roman triumphs when the all-conquering hero could all too easily begin to feel godlike as the chants of the crowd over-boosted his ego. It was the job of the slave in the back seat of the chariot to whisper in the hero's ear that he was only a mortal man when all was said and done.

However, anyone who imagines that such a difficult role is within every deputy's grasp should think again. It can take years of accumulated wisdom to develop the required presentation skills which will ensure effective performance at the appropriate time. Judging from the subsequent actions of some of the Roman heroes, the back seat chariot drivers often weren't too clever in this role either.

Blindfolding the second fiddle

ACTING AS devil's advocate to the head can be tricky on some occasions, as I indicated in the previous chapter, but challenging the head's ideas and suggesting alternatives should be an essential part of the deputy's functions. The dangers of managers colluding together to block out awkward questions and possible pitfalls have been well exemplified as 'group-think' by Irving Janis. He used, among others, the historical example of the discussions in President John F. Kennedy's management team which led to the abortive invasion of Cuba in the Bay of Pigs fiasco. Janis's argument, based on the evidence at his disposal, is that the members of the team went in for a form of self-censorship in deference to the new President so that he was not faced with the kind of critical analysis which might have sensibly led him to abandon the plans to invade. As Janis expressed it:

'When a group of people who respect each other's opinions arrives at a unanimous view each member is likely to feel that the belief must be true. This reliance on consensus validation tends to replace individual critical thinking and reality testing, unless there are clear-cut disagreements among the members. The members of a face to face group often become inclined, without realising it, to prevent latent disagreements from surfacing, when they are about to initiate a risky course of action.'[1]

Or, as Michael Dixon puts it in compiling his 'Laws of Organisational Stupidity', people in groups take decisions which individually they know are stupid. Dixon calls this the 'Abilene Paradox'.

Crisis control

Kennedy at least had the sense to learn from his mistakes. When the Cuban missile crisis loomed up, less than a year later, he selected a crisis control team in which he encouraged open discussions, and he deliberately stayed away from some of their meetings so the team as a whole would have to take ownership of, and responsibility for, the decisions they recommended. The recent analysis of the 'Kennedy tapes' of those meetings has done much to reinstate his historical reputation as a president who was a wise chairman in a situation which could very easily have degenerated into nuclear conflict.

A good headteacher should actually value the kind of openness which allows deputies and others on SMTs to cast doubt on the wisdom of his or her proposals – although it is also true that in the rare SMT which is overly critical, or even hostile, it may be advisable for heads and deputies to have signed a mutual non-aggression pact as far as the public arena is concerned (making total frankness in private even more essential).

Praise and blame

What very few heads will ever countenance is the public triumph of the deputy. The standard rule in this context is that it is the head who takes the praise and the deputy who takes the blame. Deputies would be well advised to remember this at all times. (Spokespersons for John Prescott – and perhaps more especially, even though he doesn't hold the official deputy post, Gordon Brown – also please note.)

This may well be one of the reasons why Peter Ribbins[2] wrote the following about the heads involved in a recent research project:

'Relatively few remember their days as a deputy headteacher with overwhelming enthusiasm, or the head(s) with whom they worked at the time with unqualified warmth.' Ribbins detailed the frustrations which many of these heads found during their time in the deputy role (it is, however, important to note that his sample consisted entirely of the kind of people who obviously intended to go on from doing the deputy's job to running their own show; the deputy role may be inordinately frustrating for such personality types). Their ideal seemed to be a genuine partnership between heads and deputies, where from both sides the management of the school was seen as a team effort.

The notion that becoming a deputy head is merely entering a transit camp to headship is deeply flawed, by the way, not only because not all deputies will become (or even want to become) heads, but because it can lead to an estimation of the deputy's job as not being a role which might have long-term career potential for the individual concerned. This kind of under-valuation may become a self-fulfilling prophecy.

There is a fascinating study of the group dynamics of string quartets [3] which makes you very aware of why the metaphor of 'playing second fiddle' is so powerful and so often used. It is a very tricky role indeed, but some can play it very skilfully indeed, and make it a worthwhile long term career option if they are conscious that they lack the qualities needed to be a first violinist.

Delegation

To pursue, however, the earlier analogy of managing as a team, one of the best services a deputy can perform for a head is to be a safe pair of hands when it comes to delegation. A run of dropped chances in the slips and the captain's peace of mind may be gone forever. A head has to be sure that any task delegated to the deputy will be handled with initiative and flair, but also with care. The very worst thing the deputy can do if a mistake is made is to attempt to conceal it from the head's eyes. If the head does discover the deputy's cover-up it will mean not just lost peace of mind but entry into the dark valley of deep distrust.

This, as they used to say in the B-Westerns of my youth, is a box canyon with no exit. Total mutual trust as far as the job is concerned is the most vital element in the effective head/deputy partnership. On the head's side that means avoiding the temptation to be constantly looking over the deputy's shoulder in excessive anxiety about whether the job is being done properly or not. Nothing is more likely to convince deputies that they aren't trusted or that they are not being given genuine autonomy within their delegated spheres.

To switch the team analogy from cricket to soccer, I have read nothing sadder in recent years than Brian Clough's dedication of his autobiography to the late Peter Taylor, in recognition of how much he owed to Taylor as his deputy in a management partnership which resulted in two relatively small and unfashionable football clubs achieving more (and in the second case far more) than even their most loyal fans could ever have expected. The dedication of Clough's book reads as follows:

For Peter

Still miss you badly. You once said: "When you get shot of me there won't be as much laughter in your life." You were right.

The poignancy of this is that it is to a former deputy with whom, as far as I can make out from the book, Clough had hardly been on speaking terms for the last seven years or so of Taylor's life. Once the trust between them had broken down, there was no way they could ever have rejoined forces as they had at earlier points in their careers. (Any reader, by the way, who is thinking I should be reading more educative literature at my time of life, underestimates the insights to be gained from reading frank revelations of the managerial trade from someone who has now retired from the job. To put it bluntly, any retired manager has a much reduced vested interest in being economical with the truth, at least about inter-personal relationships at work. I thoroughly recommend Clough's book to managers in any sphere, including education – and, anyway, do *you* try to control what your sons buy you for Christmas?)

Yet, at its zenith, the Clough-Taylor managerial partnership was one where the manager could trust his deputy to take decisions on the latter's own initiative in key areas of concern to both of them. What is more, Taylor could do his vital job in ways which apparently brought smiles and laughter into the manager's life.

Sense of humour

How many heads and deputies are conscious of having fun these days? No head wishing to avoid nervous breakdowns should have a deputy without a sense of humour, but unfortunately this critical lack often goes undetected at interviews. There is a very rough and ready humour indicator any interviewers can try out for themselves. For years I have asked candidates at interview whether they can recall some incident they have found amusing in their working lives, which they think (a) they could share and (b) might now amuse the panel. Incidents recounted by some candidates are both funny and revealing, but other candidates are somewhat nonplussed by what I accept can be a difficult question to respond to at interview. Some people may indeed think such a question is 'unfair', but I have yet to hear a convincing reason why.

I have both been a deputy and had deputies working for me over my years in higher education, and my experience and my reading equally suggest that the strengths and weaknesses of the deputy role are very similar both inside and outside schools. If I ask myself what is the best service the head can supply to a deputy, I am sure the answer is a constant flow of suitably edited (but not censored) information which nevertheless gives as full a picture as necessary of the total operation. Not only does this provide for the time when the head is unavoidably out of action for a spell, it also empowers deputies to take executive action whenever it is called for at their level. In effect, it allows deputies to play a shared leadership role, not just an administrative-cum-managerial one.

As long as executive actions are reported back to the head in due course so that the latter is kept fully in the picture, there should be no need, in most cases, to clear them in advance. But again this requires trust. Too many insecure leaders in all kinds of organisations feel so threatened in their interpersonal relationships that they use information power as a way of shoring up their fragile egos, preferring to keep subordinates in the dark on as many key issues as possible. If this happens in schools it introduces an element of mistrust into the head/deputy relationship which is detrimental for all concerned. Any head who goes down this road will pay a very high price in lost opportunities for teamwork. It's even harder to play second fiddle if you're blindfolded most of the time.

References
1 Janis I.L. (1972), *Victims of Group Think*. Houghton Mifflin
2 Ribbins P. (1997), 'Heads on Deputy Headship' in *Educational Management and Administration* Vol. 25 (3) pp. 295-308
3 Murnighan J.K. and Conlon D.E. (1992), 'The dynamic of intense work groups: A study of British string quartets' in *Managing Change in Education: Individual and organisational perspectives* by Bennett N, Crawford M. and Riches C. (Eds). Paul Chapman

Deviant definitions

IN HIS FAMOUS, not to say notorious, book *The Devil's Dictionary,* the American writer Ambrose Bierce, who 'disappeared' in Mexico at the age of 71 in 1913, gave new definitions to familiar words. For those unfortunate enough not to be familiar with the book, here are a couple of examples of the way Bierce's mind worked, with apologies for the sexism of his time in history:

Confidant, Confidante, *n.*
One entrusted by A with the secrets of B, confided by *him* to C.

Consolation, *n.*
The knowledge that a better man is more unfortunate than yourself.

These brief extracts from one page of this satirist's masterpiece are enough by themselves to expose the myth that the American literary mind is incapable of expressing irony. Nor do I think readers should quickly dismiss Bierce's definitions as negative cynicism. What Bierce is quarrelling with in general, I would argue, is not the particular concept behind the word or term, but the way it has become corrupted in use. To use another writer's terminology, 'partnership', for example, is a good word, but it keeps bad company. In a paradoxical fashion, I think we can reclaim the value and the 'purity' of these concepts for future generations by exposing how they have become contaminated through the use made of them by the confidence tricksters and snake-oil sellers of our times. The education road show seems to have acquired an increasing number of these latter hangers-on in recent years, so it might be worthwhile to devise our own version of the Devil's Dictionary.

A Devil's Dictionary for education management

The following are just an opening selection which come readily to my mind (readers may wish to send in their own favourites as we build up the collection towards dictionary proportions):

Accountability, *n.*
The opposite of collegiality (q.v.); in other words, the heresy that in organisations one is accountable for one's own actions. The folly of this approach is best expressed by one W. Shakespeare: "Use every man after his desert, and who should 'scape whipping?"

Appraisal, *n.*
1. Performance review system enabling line managers to identify the developmental needs of staff and provide appropriate opportunities for personal and professional growth.
2. Performance review system enabling line managers to make a systematic record of staff failures, incompetence and infringements of regulations, with a view to preparing a dossier to supply grounds for dismissal.

Collegiality, *n.*
An organisational system whereby you trust that your errors, blunders, and general incompetence will be covered and hidden from public gaze under the cloak of anonymity of committee decision-making. Your colleagues will collude in this in the fervent hope that you will do the same for them when it's their turn to

escape accountability (q.v.).

Community, *n.*
(As in community school, community education etc.) A modern equivalent of what the Americans used to call 'Joe Public' – that is to say, a heterogeneous and fluid mixture of warring factions. In our increasingly pluralistic, not to say fractured, society, these are at best temporary coalitions from that vocal part of the local citizenry which wants schools to reflect that particular set of their values which they see as under threat this week.

Delayering, *v.*
Saving money by reducing middle management posts and expecting others to carry the resulting additional burdens of administration, etc. for no extra pay.

Devolution, *n.*
The temporary delegation from the centre of those aspects of authority and responsibility that senior management currently thinks it can't be bothered with.

Downsizing, *v.*
Making some staff redundant and overworking those remaining in post.

Efficiency savings, *n.*
Financial cuts.

Empowerment, *n.*
Cosmetic make-up applied by management to hide the wrinkles of their ultimate hierarchical domination on any issue which really matters – hence apparently giving greater powers of decision making to those who weren't previously rewarded financially for managerial responsibilities, and won't be under the new regime either.

Flat managerial structures, *n.*
Delayering (q.v.).

GIGO (garbage in, garbage out), *n.*
This applies to a lot more than computer inputs and outputs in education management.

Independent consultants' report, *n.*
The justification for unpleasant decisions taken (but not promulgated) by management *before* calling in the consultants. Pleasant decisions are, by definition, taken by the management itself without any need for consultants.

Kaizen, *n.*
1. Entirely laudable system of continuous improvement designed to maintain and develop quality output by staff who feel ownership (q.v.) of their work processes.
2. Meaningless mantra chanted by managers who wouldn't know their kai from their zen.

Loyalty, *n.*
Sacrificing one's career prospects in order to boost those of others.

Management by walking about, *n.*
Snooping.

Moral standards, *n.*
Subjective criteria which are always described as slipping, falling or collapsing (depending on the degree of optimism of the commentator) from those high levels of yesteryear. In the yesteryear usually referred to these correlated very neatly with, for example, high levels of rickets, child prostitution and the disease then referred to as consumption (in modern usage, 'consumption' is an entirely different kind of disease). There is evidence that indices such as these are once again on the upturn, which makes it all the more puzzling that moral standards are apparently still declining. Education in schools is, therefore, clearly to blame.

Ownership, *n.*
A condition supposed, for no obvious reason, to be experienced by staff undergoing a process of change imposed upon them

under circumstances not of their making, by managers they do not know, who only pay lip service to the notion of consulting them. For examples, see most instances of UK government interventions in education in the 1980s and 90s.

Parental choice, *n.*
A system whereby parents with the relevant knowledge and resources can choose to keep their offspring segregated as much as possible from the children of parents lacking the aforementioned knowledge and resources, and who are therefore in no position to exercise choice. (In Northern Ireland there is a specialist usage of the term to mean religious apartheid in education.)

Participation, *n.*
1. An organisational system whereby you, as a manager, try to involve as many staff as possible in the decision making process so that they can develop a sense of ownership (q.v.).
2. An organisational system whereby you, as a manager, try to implicate as many staff as possible in the decision making process.

You then have scapegoats readily available when decisions are seen to have had catastrophic consequences and the inevitable panic and hunt for the guilty parties ensues. This process is best summed up in the injunction 'to round up the usual suspects'.

Parity, *n.*
As in 'parity of esteem', whereby schools are ranked and resourced in a hierarchical ladder of such towering proportions that those at the bottom might as well be on a different planet to those at the top. The latest variant on this approach is to have three kinds of secondary schools called *community, foundation* and *aided.* The litmus test as to which will be at the bottom of the pile is to observe those to which no New Labour ministers' offspring will go.

PC, *n.*
1. Personal Computer
2. Political Correctness.
No education manager should be without the trappings of both of these, but the flashing screen may hide the reality in both cases.

Performance-related pay (PRP), *n.*
Financial rewards for some individuals for reasons best known to management, but completely incomprehensible to those not receiving the aforementioned rewards – hence financial disincentives for team building, sharing of ideas, quality circles etc.

Performance indicators, *n.*
Quantifiable but trivial criteria pursued by the unspeakable (thanks, Oscar) at the expense of the unquantifiable but actually significant.

Quality, *n.*
A reduction in standards brought about by efficiency savings (q.v.).

Quick and Dirty Operating Systems, *n.*
1. The origin of the shortened acronymic nickname for DOS

computer programming.
2. Most education management most days.

Rightsizing, *v.*
Downsizing (q.v.).

School-based teacher training, *n.*
An apprenticeship model designed to legitimise the weak position of teachers as employees and still further undermine their claims to professional status (colloq: sitting next to Nelly most of the time).

School-centred teacher training, *n.*
The more complete severance of the links between teaching and higher education (colloq: sitting next to Nelly practically *all* of the time).

School mission statements, *n.*
In too many cases, updated versions of the old school mottoes, which were probably in dead languages unintelligible to the majority, and certainly handed down from the authorities of years long gone. Current best practice strongly suggests that mission statements should be intelligible documents, regularly reviewed and, if needs be, revised, following genuine consultation and participation at grass roots levels. School managers please note that this means bottom-up as well as top-down management.

Site-based management, *n.*
The devolution (q.v.) to school managers of decisions as to where to make the financial cuts, staff reductions etc. demanded by management based further and further away from the site. This has certain similarities with the now almost archaic expression 'passing the buck', but this tended to be a movement *upwards* – hence the sign in President Truman's office which stated 'the buck stops here'. Nowadays that would be the least likely place the buck would ever stop as it hurtled on its downward trajectory.

WYSIWYG (what you see is what you get), *n.*
1. Advances in computer software which mean that the characters you type on your PC (q.v.) screens are displayed almost identically to the printout (also known as Graphic Mode).
2. The use of smoke and mirrors in the dark arts of education management to create an impression of openness and transparency which hides the sinister and opaque reality. In education management, what you see is most certainly *not* what you get.

Democracy, banana style

THE FOLLOWING exchange is set in an obscure republic which has only in the last decade taken on the trappings of democracy after a long period of dictatorship. The Chairman (sic) of the Committee to Re-Elect the President (CREEP) is meeting the Education Minister (who happens to be female):

CHAIRMAN: Minister, you will be aware that we have invited you here today to see what measures you might take in your sphere of influence which will help to ensure the re-election of the President.

MINISTER: Well, I am sure that *you* will be aware that I wrote my doctoral thesis on the education system of England and Wales, and I think there are some significant lessons to be learned from the developments from 1944 to the present day in that country.

C: Having read the summary of your thesis, I take it you mean that educational measures which favour the offspring of the white middle class, but are not too blatantly biased in this direction, are the key to electoral success?

M: That's a crude but essentially accurate summary, yes.

C: But we already have an equivalent private system where our wealthy élite, to which we both have the good fortune to belong, can ensure that its own children have a privileged education with easy access to the better jobs in our society.

M: Quite so, but unfortunately there aren't, almost by definition, enough voters in that category to ensure a democratic majority at the polls.

C: Accepting that point, and assuming we're stuck for international reasons with this democratic experiment for the foreseeable future, I return to my argument that it's the votes of the wider middle class on which we need to concentrate.

M: I don't in any way disagree. The English evidence is that it's the way that what they call 'Middle England' votes that settles the issue. Many of the great unwashed don't bother to vote anyway, even if they're on the electoral roll, and a majority of those that do follow the middle class voting pattern because it's the class they're aspiring to join.

C: So let's establish at least one of their so-called grammar schools in every fair sized town, bring in a selection process at the age of 11 or so, and then let the gap between the good and the bad schools grow wider all the time. I gather that's the scenario the previous Conservative administration was thinking of reverting to.

M: I presume you'd select by ability? For the state system it's very hard to justify overt selection by wealth to a democratic electorate. Even the English discarded that idea over 50 years ago.

C: Naturally. After all, I understand that the statistical evidence is quite conclusive that selection by 'ability' inevitably favours the white middle class in any case.

M: Again true, but there is a fatal flaw in both your analysis and that of those Conservatives who were thinking along those lines.

C: Oh yes? And what's that?

M: The problem with that system is that there is a surprisingly large minority of middle class children who aren't as bright as the most able from poor homes. This means that inevitably some middle class children in England actually failed their 11+ examination and were not selected for grammar schools. Consequently, they were in real danger of spending their teenage years in schools with the 'roughs'. Many middle class parents weren't over-concerned about the odd one or two roughs being around when their children were very young, but they weren't going to accept it at the secondary stage if they could help it.

C: So that must have been a bit of a downer for the middle class parents of the 'failures'?

M: That's putting it mildly. There were some who couldn't afford to send their children to private schools to avoid their children having contact with the roughs, and even some of those who *could* pay resented having to fork out the cash. Worse than that, there was a lot of anxiety among the *majority* of the middle class affected each year in the period leading up to the selection. So, despite all the later propaganda to the contrary, it was a significant proportion of these people who were initially influential in supporting the move towards a comprehensive system.

C: But they were against it later on?

M: Up to a point, Lord Copper, as their tragicomic writer Evelyn Waugh puts it. They were only against it when their teenage sons and daughters had to actually sit in classes with what they saw as the local 'yobbos'.

C: Why didn't that happen from the start?

M: Because the practices of streaming and setting, with which I'm sure you're familiar, meant that the white middle class children could be fairly effectively segregated *within* the school.

C: Ah. So what was the problem?

M: Unfortunately the research evidence made this all too apparent, and some do-gooders started what they called 'mixed-ability' classes. This wasn't anything near as widespread as people imagined but, as ever, it was the fear that it *might* happen which was the cruncher, because it made segregation very difficult indeed.

C: I can see that. So why didn't they just ban this?

M: I can see you still have a lot to learn about democracy. You've got to be a lot subtler than that. You can put out a lot of negative propaganda, and you can put the frighteners on heads who take their schools down those roads, but at the end of the day there are always some potential martyrs who will follow what they laughingly refer to as their conscience or their principles.

C: That does present something of a problem.

M: Too true. The powers that be were forced to find some ways of keeping schools themselves sufficiently differentiated to allow the middle class to feel they had an adequate choice of the 'right' schools for their children.

C: How did they go about doing that?

M: Letting market forces rip in the housing market was a big help for starters. It meant that the price gap between housing in the desirable suburbs and elsewhere became an almost unbridgeable gulf. This meant you could have neighbourhood comprehensives which simply reflected the social class of the area in which they were sited.

C: That sounds OK. So why was there an issue?

M: Unfortunately some of the bigger comprehensives took in children from too wide a geographical area to make this solution yobbo-proof.

C: So what else could they do?

M: Well, the Conservatives brought in new categories of school which they called Grant Maintained schools and City Technology Colleges, where they could lavish resources at the expense of the other schools. They also allowed secondary schools to select up to 15% of their intake on ability and to interview parents before admitting their children. Add to all that the fact that it was possible to become a 'specialist' school and select up to 10% of pupils according to their so-called aptitude for particular subjects, and you can see that there was ample leeway to make some secondary schools a good deal more equal than others, to quote George Orwell. Indeed, the more equal you made some, the very less equal you made others.

C: You really do go a bundle on their writers, don't you?

M: I think few countries have provided more fertile ground for the growth of satire.

C: Yes, but what about when the Conservatives were actually defeated in an election and Labour came to power? Did their education policies have anything to do with this?

M: Only in the sense that they didn't promise to change a lot. There was some rhetoric before the election about 'no selection', but in fact those schools which were already selecting up to 15% by ability were allowed to carry on doing so 'unless challenged' by local parents, etc. You have to remember that the so-called New Labour Party was now run by people who'd also recognised that the key to electoral success was to appeal to the middle class even more than the Conservatives did. Their Prime Minister,

Tony Blair, began referring to the 'moderate, middle-income majority' as soon as he became party leader, and it was quite clear that it was their votes he was principally aiming for. So the principle of 'parental choice of school', which underpinned most of what I've been describing, was retained and even extended in some respects by New Labour. They also endorsed the idea of 'magnet schools' which in the USA were supposed to raise the achievement of their pupils, but which in reality tended to do this at the expense of the schools surrounding them.

They even built this specialist school idea into their plans for Education Action Zones, which show every sign of adding to the inegalitarian agenda. The only thing New Labour has done to reverse the trends I've mentioned has been to tell schools they shouldn't interview parents – although church schools were still allowed to do this to probe denominational allegiances (which obviously gave them scope to probe a good deal more than that). Anyway, cutting back on parental interviews suited many 'Middle Englanders' just fine because it was a bit much to think the school might fail *you* rather than your child!

C: So they may have toned down some of the more blatant anti-egalitarian measures but they retained the essentials. Weren't there *any* protests about all this on behalf of the underclass?

M: The chairman of what they call their Commission for Racial Equality did protest in rather strong terms about Labour's plans for cosmetic name changes to divide up the secondary sector into 'foundation, aided and community schools'. However, what he was essentially doing was blowing the gaff on behalf of the ethnic minorities who would be likely to lose out particularly badly in this system. He claimed that Labour's new education bill would establish 'a fractured education system, concentrating resources in high status schools, and concentrating pupils with greatest needs in schools of low status and low resources that will become seen as "sink" schools.' This was in direct contradiction to the mantras which the New Labour politicians were chanting, such as 'standards not structures' and 'social disadvantage is no excuse for low standards in schools', etc. You will readily see the attraction of such slogans for politicians who do not wish to go in for the kind of radical reform that might upset some of the vested interests of Middle England.

C: We've never been silly enough to create bodies which give a public platform to people like this CRE chairman, I'm glad to say. There are surely limits to this 'freedom of speech' idea? Nevertheless, he does actually seem to have summed up the planned situation very neatly. That will surely appeal to the majority of middle class parents. I suppose what you're telling me is that, as far as education is concerned, you can't go wrong in electoral terms in a modern democracy by giving the middle class what they want. The only thing you have to watch out for is that the opposition doesn't promise them even more of a good thing.

M: Got it in one!

Acknowledgement
Part of the inspiration for this article came from a paper by Dr. Richard Hatcher in the journal *Race, Ethnicity and Education* Vol. 1(2) October 1998 entitled 'Social Justice and the Politics of School Effectiveness and Improvement'.